Scandal in the Courtroom
Found Guilty Without Trial

D1563041

by
Grant Dinehart Langdon

CONTENTS

FOREWORD:
SCANDAL IN THE COURTROOM

Ladybug, ladybug, fly away home, your house is on
fire, your children will burn.

                —Anon, Nursery Rhyme

I had the same fear that farmers all up and down the valley had.
I was awakened by the crackling of a raging fire and a strange
glow on the bedroom wall. It is followed by the wail of the fire
siren.

If it is your barn that burns, your animals, your equipment,
and your labor go up in smoke. Your first thought is that it has
to have been an accident, no one could do this to you. Even before the fire company starts to roll up their hoses and pack them
away, you walk past the embers, past the mound of smoldering
hay you worked so hard to put up. You walk past your blackened
twisted equipment. You were still making payments on some of
it. Then you wonder where will you milk the cows in the morning? Where will you get the feed to feed the cows? Some of your
neighbors come forward and somehow you manage. Then over
the next day or two reality sets in. It is the third barn fire this
year. They are all late at night. The others also seemed suspicious
although the official word was it was "electrical."

The Copake area is in the heart of the Hudson River Valley
in upstate New York. Slowly the people of Copake realized the
truth, just as I did. Copake had a serial arsonist. Then the fear set
in. When will he make his next strike? Who will be next?

The fires started about 1980. After a fire the anger wells up
deep inside; that is if it is your first fire. I wasn't awakened like
that but this was my third barn fire and I was damned mad.

Right after my second fire I placed an ad in the August 29,
1985 edition of the Roe Jan Independent. It was in a boldly out-
lined box and read; "I would like to thank all the fireman for putting out the fire and all my friends and neighbors for the help
over the last few days. I feel fortunate to live in a community with
such kind and caring people." I signed it as Mike Langdon.

After my third fire my mood changed to outrage. Three fires were enough. We were under attack. I refused to stand idly by while the sheriff dithered, carried out ineffectual investigations, and labeled every fire cause as being electrical. I decided to strike the problem head on. I started the Stop Arson Fund soliciting information to the indictment and conviction of the arsonist. It put pressure on the sheriff, but the goal was to get the community to agree we had a problem. I wanted to generate community wide involvement. Someone knew something and we needed his or her help.

THE FATE OF THE BARN WAS SEALED

The rear door at the Bull Spring barn hung open on the east-west wing of the L-shaped barn outside of Copake. In the hay-mow, chopped cornstalks were piled up for use in the stable below on the east end. That is where the fire started.

High above the floor and the cornstalks on the north wall was a small open door. On the west end there was a small amount of hay with an open door to the north just above the ground. Conditions were ideal. Air movement was good.

About 8:00 P.M. Fran Dick came out on the porch to sit and enjoy the perfect evening. She did not sit there long when she noticed a wisp of smoke coming over the roof of the old horse barn next to the road. She walked over to the driveway to get a better look at the cow barn.

"The Barn's on fire!" she shouted, and ran back inside to call for help. Bill Carrel was tending his small garden nearby. When Bill heard Fran he headed to the driveway to get a better look. White smoke was coming from the little door on the east end of the barn. He too headed back to call for help. Back inside Fran was already talking to Fire Control when she heard a blast. The time recorded by Fire Control was 8:06 P.M. Larry Dick rushed out to look. Fire was blasting out of the north door in the direction of the corncrib across the driveway.

The Lilly family lived a short distance away and was picnicking on the lawn when the spotted the black smoke rising. Fire sirens rent the air. Only minutes later Fire Chief Randy Shadic, who lived nearby, assessed the situation. No water was close by. He would have to set up a holding tank and organize the arriving trucks to carry water. Firemen were arriving in cars. Most of the fire was on the north end of the barn. It had died back and was now simply curling up under the eves. Randy ordered the corncrib fire put out. The fate of the much larger cow barn was already sealed.

As soon as I learned the fire was at Bull Spring Farm I headed out as fast as the car could go. After I rounded the curve at Brown's Dam I sped up again just as I noticed half a dozen cars and people watching the fire along Snyder Pond Road. One man seemed to be standing in my pasture watching the fire. Then the barn came into view. My heart sank and my anger rose. I knew it had to be arson. I headed to the south wing of the barn since there was no fire in that wing yet. I started to free the calves.

Scott Hedges showed up in his fire gear. He said, "Get out of there. You can't be in there." I kept freeing the calves. Frank showed up and helped. Finally Scott pitched in and all the calves were saved. After the calves were freed Scott, Frank and the other firemen helped save as much as we could from the milk house and silo room. Then I walked around the barn, trying to assess the damage. "Who the Hell did this?" I ranted. "It's got to be a fireman!"

HOW BEAUTIFUL CAN THE TRUTH BE, WHEN IT'S KILLING YOU?

> "I loved the farm, my friends, and the upstate village of Copake. I never doubted that I would live my whole life on the farm surrounded by people I knew and trusted. That was before the fires changed my life."
> —Grant "Mike" Dinehart Langdon

We all have a special place, a place where we look back on our lives and chart the future. I had A.D.'s desk. It is the same desk I am sitting behind in Cincinnati, Ohio. Here, I have that and a few pictures of my past. When I look back on these memories, I hear the melody of my heritage and my life in Copake. A.D. was my grandfather. His desk and a few pictures are tangible reminders of how much I was both enriched and impoverished in life.

A.D. was a superhero, not just to me, but also to all who knew him. He was tall, thin, dignified and generous. He wore a neatly trimmed mustache and was always neatly dressed. He not only carried a cane but also loved a big cigar. You could feel his presence when he walked in, smiling, his eyes twinkling. And, he always had a good word to say. His outgoing personality commanded respect from everyone who met him. We all simply called him, "A.D." A.D. coined the name "Langdonhurst Farm" and combined several farms into a 2,000-acre operation in the Twenties. He lived in a big house with a view of the village as well as a panorama of the farms. Everyone knew he would be there for them if needed, and he was in tune with the town and the times.

A.D. loved Copake and helped start the fire company back in the Twenties. He also donated land for the cemetery. When the Great Depression hit, A.D. helped his neighbors. He gave many of them jobs, and he helped others by giving them loans. He liked people and had a great sense of humor. One story he enjoyed telling made him the butt of a joke.

He was just one of the boys when a group of local men, all his friends, suggested they get together and have a chicken roast.

A.D. was game for the adventure. They decided to hold it at Benton's Cove on the old millpond. It was a pleasant summer's evening, and the place was perfect for getting away from the daily chores. The trick was that someone's chicken house had to be raided.

A.D., not too sure he wanted to get caught stealing someone's chickens, offered to be in charge of getting firewood, getting the fire started and heating the water needed to pick the chickens. The others, apparently unfazed about the possibility of getting caught, went marauding for the chickens.

A.D. was just finishing his chicken when he remarked at how good the chicken was. "They ought to be," one of his friends quipped, "we got them out of your chicken house." No one laughed harder than Grandpa. He was proud of how well his chickens grew that year, but he didn't brag about how well his chickens grew after that.

AMERICA THE BEAUTIFUL

My own farm was in the family for over a hundred years. I loved going up on the big hill behind my barn to check on the crops, especially as evening approached. A deep connection to the rich limestone loam, some of the best growing soil in the county, warmed my heart. I loved looking east over the valley at the rugged Taconic Hills with the sun at my back. In the fall, the colors were simply beautiful.

Over to my left, the 1854 Methodist Church gleamed in the sunlight with its Greek revival columns. It stands out in the scattering of houses and small business buildings that comprise the hamlet of Copake. All before me, the valley fields of golden grain and lush corn soak up the slanting sunlight. On the far side of the valley Pearson's brilliant red barn is a jewel-like exclamation against the illuminated mountains. To the north, the Bash Bish gorge cuts deep into the mountains. I could never take in all this beauty without thinking of the song I first learned in the two-room schoolhouse on the edge of the hamlet. "America the Beautiful" became and remains my anthem of love for this country.

World War II ended, and optimism began to replace the pessimism lingering from war rationing and the Depression. The two-story watchtower, manned by the community to spot enemy planes swooping down the valley toward New York City, stood empty. Route 22 threaded its way up the Harlem Valley from Millerton, and after years of neglect the roadway was rough and hard to travel. Just north of Millerton, the low, rugged Taconic Hills marked New York's border with Connecticut and then Massachusetts on the east. On the west, steep hills give way to rolling hills and the farmland of Columbia County. A few miles north of Millerton, Route 22 turned abruptly east to dip down into Boston Corners before heading north again to where the valley widened past more farms.

At Dean's flats, the road turned west going past Borden's milk plant and Bristol's feed store. The Borden's plant had refrigeration and shipped milk to the city by truck. Before that, it was shipped by rail to Poughkeepsie and on to New York on the tracks that ran adjacent to the plant. The Borden plant was at the economic heart of the town, and farmers brought their milk there in heavy lidded milk cans where two men lugged them up onto the platform to be tested. They would pry the lids off and smell of the milk. That was the test. If it smelled okay, the milk was dumped into a vat that in turn fed the bottling equipment. If the milk was "bad," the farmer took it home and fed it to the pigs. Sometimes the amount of "bad" milk seemed to be governed by demand

Before refrigeration the milk was cooled by ice. Borden's ran an icehouse and hired farmers to come with teams of horses to fill it. The ice was harvested off Benton Cove on Robinson Lake, or Brown's Pond as we called it. Filling the icehouse was a big event that involved timing with the weather and pay for the men and their teams of horses. The noon meal on these occasions became the focus of the community, and a fire was built at the edge of the cove. All the wives gathered to visit and prepare the noon meal.

Farther up Route 22, you came to the Copake Theater and Harvey Roberts' Chrysler-Plymouth car dealership. Route 22 carried a steady stream of travelers from New York City through the center of town on Main Street, and the dining room at the Holsapple House was always busy with overnight guests. The church, Hedges Store, Fuller's Store, the Drug Store and the barbershop filled out the center of town. Further up Route 22, just past Dean's dairy barn, the 1920's firehouse set close to the road with its upstairs meeting rooms. Up the street, Fred Link built his frozen food locker and sold appliances. Around the sharp corner you came to Folger's, the old garage where Henry Folger started his auction business, and across from the auction house, Pete Miles started his lumber business in Wally Funk's old cow barn. From there, Route 22 twisted its way to the busy hamlet of Copake Falls on the edge of the state park. There, you might meet Foster Ham, taxi man. Foster met one of the five express trains to New York on the Harlem division of the New York Central. He was always busy in the summer until a new road bypassed Boston Corners, Copake and Copake Falls. In ten years the trains no longer stopped, and road traffic dropped off, too, with the extension of the Taconic State Parkway to the west.

Our main dairy barn was at the west end of Church Street just beyond the sidewalk. A second barn, the McGee barn, was near the end of Church Street. When all the work was done with the horses, A.D. kept 14 teams in the McGee barn. I walked to school past our big barn to the gravel Center Hill Road. After I turned right, it was a short distance up Church Street to where the sidewalk and cement road began. The blacktop county road made a sharp corner from West Copake and Ancram and met Church Street. The sidewalk started at John Lind's house, right across the driveway from A.D.'s big house. On the north side of the sidewalk, I only went past eight houses before passing the cemetery and the Methodist Church near Hedges store and the center of town. Our McGee barn, Grandma Carry's house and small orchard stood on the south side.

Grandma Carry, A.D.'s mother, was widowed young when her storekeeper husband, Grant, died in 1899. Aunt Millie Link was her live-in housekeeper, and I always looked forward to stopping in after Sunday school to get one of Aunt Millie's molasses cookies. Although Aunt Millie wasn't really an aunt, she assumed the title because of her position in the household. She was a small, hard-working woman, bent with age, and she would take

us back to the old-fashioned kitchen where she let us climb the
two steps to the cool pantry. Under a heavy plate covering a
stoneware crock, moist molasses cookies awaited our anxious
fingers.

Just past Grandma Carry's orchard came Dr. Bowerhan's
house, the funeral parlor and Buel Peck's place. Charlie Peck
lived over the funeral parlor and his son Brad lived across the
street on the west side. Brad was just opening his insurance business next to Frank's garage, and I crossed the street to the Holsapple House and followed the sidewalk down the dirt road past
the Grange Hall to the two-room grade school. The other grades
went to Roe Jan Central School, six miles north in Hillsdale.

The Grange Hall and the Copake Theater were centers of
activity, and before television, people came from miles around
to take in shows at the theater. For me, it was a treat to see
other kids and neighbors. Jesse and Rose Head might be there.
Jesse was a towering big man who chewed tobacco and liked
kids. He grew up on his father's farm just down the dirt road
past the school.

"Just a minute," he'd say, "I gotta knife here, how about a
swap?" He would thrust his hand into his pocket and draw out a
closed fist. You'd be faced with the dilemma of getting rid of that
old knife of yours with the bent blade or keeping it. His knife
might have a real bone handle and steel blade, or, maybe not.
After you made the swap, you wondered how he could even call
his piece of junk a knife. I soon learned to keep two knives in my
pocket, one to use, one to swap.

Jesse might tell you a great story from his childhood, like
when he rode with my grandfather Fischer. He was Supervisor
of the neighboring town of Ancram. Carl Fischer was great fun
for the kids before he died in the flu epidemic of 1919.

You were likely to run into Jesse at the Grange or between
shows at the theater, and the theater was a community magnet
visited by nearly everyone. Eddy McIntyre and Ina Ferguson,
Eddy's sister, ran the Copake Theater. Their father, Steven, ran a
store across the street from my great grandfather's store in the
center of the village. The McIntire's began showing movies in the
Grange Hall in the Twenties. Those were the days of silent
movies, and Eddy played the piano. He was good at it and enjoyed improvising new music for each scene. He really seemed

to enjoy life, too. When talkies hit the screen in the 1930s, they built the theater building and closed the store.

I remember the old McIntyre store as an empty but interesting building bordering the wide swing of Route 22. In its day it was the busiest store in Copake. Across the front of it was an open porch, and one time my curiosity drew me across the street to peer into the dusty, dirty windows. Along both walls I saw clerks manning long, low counters.

A.D. enjoyed telling a story about a large, heavy man they called "Fred." Fred liked to come into Steven's store and sit on the counter, which annoyed Steven to no end. He asked Fred not to sit on the counter, but it didn't seem to register. The counter, worn by time, had a crack in it. One slow business afternoon, Steven rigged a hatpin with sticks and a rubber band so that he could snap the pin through the crack by pulling a string. When Fred came in and plopped on the counter, Steven pulled the string sending the pin perfectly through the crack. Fred reacted by sliding off the counter. That proved to be a bad move, because the pin did extra damage to his ample rear-end. The entire town heard about the incident and Fred was reminded of it for years. Nobody else ever sat on that counter either.

The McIntire's were one of the leading families in Copake. One of the first big events I remember was the return from the European war of Eddy and Ina's brother Steven for burial. Everyone showed up to pay his or her respects. Steven's loss was a tragedy for the family and the entire community. I remember the big military funeral, the flag-draped coffin, the rifle-fire salute, the bugle sounding "Taps" in the background. The McIntyre family gave a clock to the village and dedicated it to Steven and all the youth who died in the war. It replaced the flagpole and a small, painted wooden monument listing the names of veterans of past wars. The cement base for the flagpole had to be dug out by a bulldozer. I remember following along behind the dozer with other kids as it pushed the mass down the dirt road past the Grange, the school, and right across our field to the Bash Bish brook. Had Steven returned, the store might have gone on.

About the Author

Grant Dinehart Langdon was born in Hudson, New York, in 1938 and grew up in Copake, New York, in the house built by his tenth great-grandfather. He graduated from Iowa State University, class of 1962 in farm operation. He returned home to take over a part of the family farm. He married Nancy Frank Wishart of Smithfield, Virginia, in 1963 and they had three children. His first marriage ended in divorce in 1980.

He soon became president of Columbia County Farm Bureau and, as such, organized a North East Dairy Day in 1978 that attracted the Governor of New York and the United States Secretary of Agriculture as principal speakers. His experience with the Dairy Day gave the author a platform to address a problem facing farmers of the state. When a milk handler went broke, their lender was seizing the accounts receivable, and the farmers were not getting paid for the milk. His proposal resulted in better bonding of milk handlers.

Soon after the Dairy Day, Copake was hit by a series of arson fires that brought terror to the rural community. The author had three barns burned by the arsonist and sensed the sheriff, either for family or political reasons, was not carrying out his duty to arrest the arsonist. He again took the lead by establishing a reward fund and publicizing the problem. After being interviewed by a reporter from the *New York Times*, the reporter confronted the sheriff and asked if a fireman failed a lie detector test. The sheriff refused to answer, but arrested the author's 19-year-old son a week later for burning the author's barn in order to to discredit the author.

Being completely discredited, he soon became embroiled in the legal process that revealed many weaknesses in the court system. He believes problems in the court are fueled by what the author calls Club Justice. Club Justice is the network of friendships that grow up between lawyer, judges, prosecutors, and so forth that result in rules of the court being overlooked. Because the charges were dropped before trial, the author's son was never cleared of the crime. The fires continued, and his son was blamed and was forced from the community. The author remarried but the effort of the author and his new wife to diversify and save the farm failed. The farm was eventually lost on the courthouse steps, and the author first took a job in a flour mill. The stress of the legal problems eventually cost the author his marriage, and he moved to Ohio in 1998 with only $200 in his pocket. He is employed at Lowe's in Cincinnati.

After the move to Ohio the fight to clear his son's name and recover damages in court continued. New problems in the court system emerged and the fight to recover damages ended. The author, after been told his story could well be made into a movie, decided to tell his story in a book. A complaint of judicial misconduct was filed but a ruling cleared the judge in 2003.

Recently, the author became aware of a study by Justice Breyer of the Supreme Court on the *Judicial Conduct and Disability Act of 1980*. One of the identified failings of the Act was that investigation, although authorized, was not done. The author pointed out it was judges investigating other judges. Because the author experienced the problem first-hand, he saw the opportunity to turn his book into a drive to improve the system. He proposes a mandatory Department of Justice investigation of all appeals to the Judicial Council before the council hears the appeal.

The author asked the District Judge to act on lawyer misconduct, yet a hearing to explore the matter was never held. When that complaint was filed with the Court of Appeals, the only investigation was the Chief Judge sent the complaint to the judge for comments. After the Chief Judge's ruling, an appeal was filed to the Judicial Council. Again, no investigation was done. Every year innocent people are convicted and sent to prison because of failures similar to abuses the author saw. The number of men freed because of new DNA evidence proves the point.

Because of his experience as Farm Bureau President, the author feels it is possible for one person the change the system. He feels this modest change in the law will influence far more that the 700 or so charges of judicial misconduct filed each year. The present system of judges investigating judges is not working. We can do better.

COPAKE IN THE FIFTIES

In the fifties the Grange Hall was the center of Copake activity. Everyone showed up at election time and ate supper at the Grange. The Boy Scouts met there and the church hosted dinners there. By that time I was a responsible farm kid with my own set of chores to do, feeding the chickens and the pigs and helping with the sheep—lambing time was a lot of fun. Occasionally, an orphan lamb had to be bottle-fed. It was always a treat to go to the Grange and meet your friends and get to know the neighbors. In the Copake I came to know and love then, our work and lives seemed intertwined, rooted in the same place.

Eventually, Copake got two banks where the community gathered to do business and trade, I can remember when we used to frequent the I. L. Hedges store to buy most of our goods and to do "banking" too. Hazel who ran the store for the family cashed the checks, but she was careful about it, especially with larger sums. She surveyed the room warily before opening the dry bean drawer where the money was kept.

At Hedges, you could also bring your vinegar jug when it needed filling. She put the jug under a small hand pump and turned the crank that tapped into the barrel in the basement. Who'd guess that the store was also the base for the plumbing business that Clayton ran. He had his business crammed into a desk in a nook off the main room; he kept the supplies in some of the outbuildings. I remember Dad explaining the technique of getting Clayton to perform plumbing jobs. For instance, if you asked Clayton to do something it might take months and repeated phone calls to hear from him, whereas a stop by the store about 7 P.M. and lengthy visit usually accomplished a timely service call. That was just the way business got done.

My great grandfather built the larger general store on the corner not long before he died. Ernest Fuller ran it back then. He didn't do as much business and as Hedges, but then Arthur Long bought the place. Arthur was a hard-working Irishman who learned the trade as an apprentice in Ireland. He always asked if you'd forgotten something when he checked you out. The practice sent you back for one more item almost every time. I sold my eggs there and used the money to buy feed at Bristol's.

According to A.D., when my great grandfather Grant ran the store, a man named Coxie helped him. "Coxie" derived from the name Wilcoxs. As the story goes, an old man by the name of Gibbie traded in the store. He stuttered quite a bit, and you had to be patient to understand him. One day Gibbie needed some medical advice.

"T-t-t-ell me, Grantie, w-w-w-what s-s-should I d-d-do for my h-h-hemorrhoids?"

Grantie, well-liked and always ready for a good time, answered without hesitation. "Put a little turpentine on them, Gibbie!"

A week passed before Gibbie returned. My great grandfather inquired about his hemorrhoids. "W-w-well, Grantie, t-t-treatment w-w-worked, but I t-t-tell you, i-i-it t-t-takes a powerful s-s-strong t-t-touch hole to s-s-stand it."

My great grandfather built the general store in 1890, after his old store burned, and before that, Grant ran a small store across the square where his business outgrew the building. He moved his goods to the new building that had served as the Methodist church before the new church was constructed in 1854. And, his business wasn't the only one in the building as F. W. Mitchell operated a barbershop on the top floor while Frank Pulver ran a salon in the basement.

HARBINGERS OF FIRE

April 25, 1889. I don't know who discovered the fire near the upstairs wood stove, but around six in the morning, a person ran to the church, dashed upstairs and rang the church bell. People filled the street. A strong east wind was hitting Copake, and there was no hope of saving the building. Usually, the mountains offer a pleasant view to the east but they are also just high enough to speed the upper winds and storms can swoop into the valley with hurricane force. That morning, every man, woman and child came out with ladders, blankets and pails. The hand pump at the horse-watering trough was put into full operation and while some carried water in pails, others strung soaked blankets on the ladders and pushed them against the walls of the tin shop and Ward Van DeBogart's barn. Others put out small fires as they started, while others rescued what goods and supplies they could carry. Since the fire started near the wood stove on the top floor, all of F. W. Mitchell's goods were lost, but because Frank Pulver's saloon was in the basement, everything was saved. The next day Frank Pulver moved to Millerton. My great grandfather lost nearly everything, but he hung on and rebuilt a short time later.

The New Store about 1895

SOCIALIZING SPICES TRADE

The drug store, two hotels, Hanks and the Holsapple House were all near the center of town. Bristol's lumberyard handled feed and fuel oil from its bays not far from the Borden's milk plant. Farmers drove their pickup trucks in to deliver the milk and then picked up feed at Bristol's. When a farmer ordered feed, a man upstairs sent the feedbags down a chute to the platform, and they were loaded onto the farmer's truck. Then the farmer pulled over, parked, paid and picked up additional supplies. While standing in line everyone got a chance to trade stories, news and gossip, usually in good humor.

The Copake Telephone Company got started by a group of men who decided the time of the telephone had come to town. They invested some money and hired the young Yale graduate, John D. Ackley to run the company, which was located in the center of town. Over time, because the phone company never paid any dividends, he bought up all the shares and "became" the phone company himself.

Everyone knew, Claris, the telephone operator. In the days of the crank phone, you could ask her to connect you to a number or a person directly. From the phone office in the center of town she had a panoramic view of comings and goings. Sometimes she was able to tell you particular people weren't home, because she had just seen them go by on their way to Great Barrington or Millerton. If anyone needed Doc Bowerhan in a hurry, Claris was likely to know where he was or where he was headed.

The Peck families owned the insurance company next to Frank's Garage, and they owned the funeral parlor a few houses down Church Street. Charlie Peck started both businesses and later turned them over to his sons, Brad and Buel. Buel, the taller of the two operated the funeral parlor and both sons lived on Church Street close to their businesses. Folger's Auction, the car dealership and the garages filled the nucleus of the town.

The Chrysler-Plymouth dealership started by Harvey Roberts did so well that he built a new garage. And, Harvey possessed a curiosity much more intriguing than the ballyhooed autumn automobile models. His left hand was missing its thumb. He accidentally cut it off with an ax while making kindling wood. It seemed to be common knowledge that Harvey had the thumb pickled and stored on a kitchen shelf, but I never met anyone who actually saw the pickled thumb.

The mainstay of Harvey's business was the chief mechanic, Andy Grau. If anything went wrong with your car, you had to talk with Andy. He was old and bald when I knew him, but Harvey's sons supported the business too, and they all did a good gas business before the Route 22 bypass took traffic around the village center.

Frank Stang's garage served the locals, however, and he gradually became a local institution. Frank lost a leg in childhood and had been selling gas since the twenties. His good nature, big smile and stiff-legged walk cut an image everyone liked. Frank was the first person who made a go of the filling station that moved into the old livery, which used to serve the Holsapple House next door. The men liked to gather at Frank's to talk hunting and farming, and you could expect a cup of coffee and lots of gossip with each fill-up. His easy-going manner and concern for others provided a comfortable environment for the far-flung independent types, and it enhanced a very successful business formula, too. Frank's big love was the New York Giants, and the kids loved to talk baseball with him. Frank's other big love was the fire company, and that made him special in the community.

That was the Copake where I grew up, where the Boy Scouts met in the Grange, where young men took their first dates to the Copake Theater, where men like Frank Stang spent a lifetime living and working with other local men and women who had known and trusted each other most of their lives. It was a rural community little noted by the city people and campers that flooded the area every summer except for its apparent charm. For people like me, it was simply home, our world, everything.

A DARKER SIDE OF PARADISE

As a farm family we worked hard and never had a great deal of money to spend. But I loved it. As the trains stopped running and the road bypassed Copake, others saw Copake differently. At about this time the paper mill in neighboring Ancram shut down for a while too. Copake now meant less opportunity and low paying jobs. It meant poverty, and a place where nothing happened. To some Copake now was a place where others had money for new clothes for the school dance. They did not. Copake was where others gathered at the Grange, and other families bought the new cars. Perhaps they didn't get to play on the basketball team. To them all that was available was the lousy farm jobs of scraping up after the cows. At the summer camps surrounding the area, they were the ones cleaning up trash, painting cabins and mowing lawns. Respectable jobs went to imports who supervised city children. To the young locals it was a world that demeaned and dominated them. Two Copakes—one still open and friendly, the other closed and indifferent. The second Copake spawned the arsonist, and it was the second Copake that changed the future of the place. Poverty has a social cost too.

The arsonist learned his trade from the fire company and, ironically, got his first public acceptance in his role as a fireman. He received his uniform, he marched in the county fair parades along side the carpenters, plumbers, telephone linemen, and even the business and farm owners. They were the very people that made it possible for him to attend fire schools where he learned the particulars of equipment care and the nature of fire. They even sent him to arson school, where he learned how to detect arson. In the process he learned how to start fires He could now challenge authority.

CAMP FIRES FIRST

It began with the camps and spread to the farms. The earliest fires I can remember date to my year in the fourth grade. On my walk along Church Street to school, my schoolmate Lillian's house showed smoke out back. The house belonged to her grandfather and several grown children lived there. The building had been used for a horse barn and they were using it to keep the car, although the car usually sat outside. There was no electricity to the barn, and Lillian's explanation was that the fire was probably started by a bum who had spent the night and let his cigarette smolder in the dry chaff.

Even at that young age, something became apparent to me. Fires offered excitement, and the community turned out not only to help in any way they could but also to visit with their neighbors and to watch the firemen at work. Being a fireman was suddenly the most important and public job in the community. Unconsciously, people could think, "What's the harm? It's only property, and someone else's at that."

A few years later, fires beset the half-dozen camps in and around Copake. The first I went to was at the Flamingo Inn. The Inn wasn't a camp, per se, but it served the summer campers until it closed for the winter. The siren blew late at night. I remember the odd looking building behind the main lodge. It had a big water tank on the third floor level. It was where receptions were held after the reconstruction following the fire.

The next fire was less than a quarter mile away in a lovely colonial house near one of the camps. The whole community responded to the late night siren. The main part of the house with all its fancy woodwork was destroyed, but the back was saved. I remember running outside and looking up for the tell-tale glow in the sky. We piled into the car and headed toward the glow, speculating on the source of the fire. We parked a distance away so we wouldn't interfere with the firemen. It was cold, and after we got a closer look, we returned to the car to get warm.

When the siren next blew in the middle of the night, the fire was in West Copake, past the Dutch Reformed Church in a Knickerbockers boarding house. Financial difficulties were rumored, so it could have been insurance or revenge that torched the place. One thing the community knew though was that the fires were intentionally set, and that they were happening more often. When the farmers delivered their milk and picked up supplies at Borden's and Bristol's, the talk was all about fires and possible arson.

The last of the big fires hit Clint Banner's barn. As was becoming typical, it started late at night and brought out the whole community. I was there with my father when he talked with Clint after the fire. The big decision was whether or not to rebuild. Although Clint was too young to retire, the insurance alone was not going to cover the cost of rebuilding. He had to assume a large debt in addition to collecting insurance money.

The firebug had struck fear into the hearts of the farming community. They saw the debt Clint took on, and they didn't want to face the same situation. Big debt is a true threat in fire. Rebuilding and rebounding are costly in obvious and material ways, but the indirect costs are enormous too. New equipment, feed and a reconstituted herd are suddenly up-front expenses and the farmer cannot use his inventory to balance the budget. I remember the supper table conversations about Alfred Silvernail's spotlights that covered his whole house, barn and yard area, how expensive it was to keep those lights burning all night. In a thrifty little community it was seen as a big expense.

The farming community was clearly not sleeping soundly. Many of the young men got drafted for duty in the Korean War, and the fires stopped. Silvernail kept his lights shining as the rest of the community gradually returned to normal.

MAKING MY WAY AS A FARMER

I worked long and hard on the farm as the years rolled by. Dad's big barn had a huge haymow that seemed impossible to empty unless there was a drought or a substandard hay crop. I remember 1955 best, because I was in Junior High School, and a lot happened. Dad let me keep a few chickens, and I was selling eggs at the general store. I took care of two pigs that we butchered in the fall, but my main job was feeding heifers and bringing in the hay during the summer.

I got to operate the John Deer, a tractor with the no. 5 mower attachment. It had a 7-foot mower bar extending from the right side of the tractor. The tractor made a "pop-pop" sound with its two-cylinder engine, and its narrow front end and hydraulic control system made it a distinct machine. Every fitting on the tractor and mower had to be greased and oiled; the mower blades had to be sharpened by hand with a file. If one of the knife guards got dinged, it caused a grass build-up, and it had to be polished with emery. When the dew dried off the field, it was time to mow.

Practice made me good at mowing. I ran the tractor at full throttle, and if I came to a woodchuck hole, the mower could be lifted in timely fashion by hitting the hydraulic control just before hitting the hole. Then, just as quickly, I'd lower it again. If my timing was off, the mower bar could pick up a stone and force a stop for a knife replacement. At a corner in the field, I pulled back on the throttle, hit the hydraulic lever, stepped on the right break pedal and steered right, all at the same time. The big wheel of the tractor stopped precisely on the corner, and the mower bar would cut into the hay at a perfect 90-degree angle without plugging up or skipping part of a swath. Then it was back to full throttle and another run down the field. Timing had to be near perfect to leave 7 feet of un-mown hay. After lunch, it was time to bale hay.

In those days Dad drove the baler and the bales dropped on the ground. Sometimes I helped pick up the hay, and sometimes I loaded bales that weighed 40 or 50 pounds, depending on their dampness. We could stack 7 tiers of bales onto a hay wagon. Grabbing the bales by the strings and lifting them up could load the first tiers, but we filled the top tiers by pitchfork. On a good day we could move 2,000 bales, or about 45 tons. I got to handle most of it twice, so by days' end I was really tired, and after a few minutes of caring for the chickens and pigs I hit the shower, ate supper, nodded at the TV and went to bed. On a Saturday I could walk into town for a movie.

The summer bronzed my body and toughened my hands. September brought silo filling time and the kind of near disaster ever threatening on the farm. We had been filling an old tile silo that was strung together by metal rods grooved through the tiles. One man worked the last of the silage in and came down to talk with a feed truck driver who'd showed up with a delivery. As they talked in front of the truck, one of the rods snapped about two-thirds of the way up the silo, and then the entire thing opened up and fell toward them. The top of the silo smashed the truck bumper as the men dodged to safety. Part of the barn was damaged, and the silo ended up being a big pile of silage and broken tile. With worse timing, one or two men could have been killed.

FIRE COMES HOME

Mid-October 1955. I remember the morning well. My hands were healed. I was settled into the school routine. Dad had just come into the house from the barn, and it was the first morning we kept the cows in, so after milking they were locked into their stanchions and fed there. Dad finished washing up and sat down at the table for his breakfast as I headed through the kitchen to catch the school bus outside. Huge billowing smoke horrified me as I rounded the corner of the house.

"THE BARN IS ON FIRE," I yelled. I dropped my books, ran to the stone wall and vaulted over and went into the barn. Smoke was coming down through the hay-shoots in the ceiling where the hay was dropped down. The cows knew something was wrong. They pulled tightly against the stanchions making it harder to release them, but as soon as the stanchions opened they ran out. I closed the hay shoot doors as I came to them. Finally the smoke thickened, and burning hay was falling through one of the shoots forcing me to retreat. I could hear somebody else releasing the cows on the other side of the fire so I raced over to the other side. By the time I got out most of the cows were saved, but flames shot high into the air. Only ten minutes, and one of the biggest barns around was fully engulfed in fire. The hay was gone; my summer's work was gone, too. Now we need to find a place to feed and milk the cows.

The emergency move for the cows took a lot of help from the farming community. A barn was located 20 miles away, and we didn't get home until near midnight. We had to make the return trip by 4 A.M. for the morning milking. Since the barn was too small for the entire herd, half of the cows were kept in a shed after milking. Hay and silage now had to be purchased to feed them. It was clear that a decision had to be made and Dad knew that meant moving part of the herd to the auction barn in Copake. The remainder of the herd continued to be milked on the rented farm site.

Everything was under control for the auction. The cows were clipped and groomed and even broken so they could be lead by rope halters. Production records for each cow were printed in the catalog along with a few pictures of show animals. Milking was timed so the cows carried full utter into the auction ring. Dad had an emotional time giving the history of the herd as the auction got underway. The first cow was lead in, and when the gavel banged for the sale, it looked good. With the big crowd and the successful sale, pressure on the farm operation eased, and the feed situation and the milking process became manageable. But the reminders of the fire persisted in the form of a mountain of smoldering hay I walked past every morning on my way to school. Its odor permeated our house and was virtually inescapable.

When spring came, Frank Stang pulled the community together in what would be the quintessential community clean-up day. Everyone showed up with equipment from front loaders to pitch forks. They came from miles around: Hillsdale, Ancram, and even Mt. Washington in western Massachusetts. A clean-up assembly line of trucks removed rotten hay and decrepit wooden beams to the town dump where a bulldozer worked to bury the rubble. I remember Harvey Young standing atop a mountain of hay with his pitchfork raised, his red shirt blazing in the sun. By the end of the second weekend, the smoke was finally gone and it was easier to sleep at night.

Although there wasn't enough insurance money to rebuild, the auction proceeds closed the financial gaps, and Dad could think about reorganizing. The farm's big chicken house got made over into a cow barn, and by the following fall, silos were raised, and our cows were transported back, ending the 20-mile milking odyssey for them and us. Recovering from the fire took a major coming together for my parents, my brother and me, but it also drew on the support of the Copake community that seemed to live by a version of the golden rule in those days. By the time I reached maturity, owned my own farm and was busy raising my own family, Copake's "golden rule" community spirit was tarnished and about to flag.

A DISTANT COUSIN OWNS THE BIG FARM

Ben Ackley owned the Empire Farm next to my land. Ben's mother and my grandmother were friends and distant cousins. Ben had a little money when the phone company his father helped start got going. Ben decided to forego raising pure-bred Holsteins to work with horses. William Dinehart owned the farm back in the 1800's. By 1890, or so, he built Empire Farm into one of the best harness-horse breeding farms in the state. Ben sold his cows, opened the fine old buildings and graded the old race-track. He kept his own horses and rented extra space in the barns to half a dozen other horse owners. They gathered early in the morning to train for the big races at Saratoga.

In the spring, matinee runs were held to test the horses, and word got out that Empire Farm was the place to enjoy a Sunday afternoon. A.D., my grandfather, loved horses and just had to be there. Claude Busset, who prided himself as an ace handicapper, wanted to bet. He urged A.D. to bet five dollars on a race. He liked a horse owned by one Harold Bruns. A.D. was hesitant about picking a horse, but Busset persisted.

Finally A.D. gave in. "All right. Pick your horse," he said. Claude picked Harold's horse.

"OK I'll bet on the field, then," A.D., said.

Busset's horse finished second, and he felt pretty sheepish handing over the money. He'd bet his one horse against the other five horses in the race.

DAIRY DAY PUTS COPAKE ON THE MAP

And the cow and the bear shall feed; their young ones
shall lie down together: and the lion shall eat straw
like an ox.

Isaiah 11:7

Our farming community finally made the big time in 1978, when Dairy Day was staged at my farm. Some important people had been invited. I was standing out by the firehouse watching the big tent go up. After two years of planning and preparing, I was feeling pretty confident it would go well. Then Sheriff Proper drove up and stopped his car near me. "How are plans going?" he asked.

"It looks good, but I don't know how many people we'll get."

"I'll have some men here, but I don't think it will amount to much," Proper chuckled. "I checked and the last time a Secretary of Agriculture came to the county, and there were only about 60 people that showed up." The sheriff drove off. I stood beside the road thinking that the sheriff was a Republican and the Secretary of Agriculture was a Democrat. I already had 100 volunteers working on the project, so I wasn't impressed with his attitude. I anticipated a successful event.

The Roe Jan Independent newspaper was a big boost with publicity and a special edition outlining the program events ran with a front-page proclamation for Northeast Dairy Day issued by Columbia County Supervisor Butch Near. It all contributed to an estimated crowd of 4,000 people, a bit above the sheriff's expectations, I'd say.

On June 27th the tents, exhibits and booths were set up. It was a very hot day. I put my old college roommate from Iowa State in charge of taking pictures and busied myself with last minute details. One of the rental trucks turned over and damaged the speaker system. With the head of milk marketing from the USDA, the Secretary of Agriculture and the Governor coming, we had to rely on somebody's personal, and smaller, speaker system. We had another problem with the late arrival of the caterer providing the chicken barbecue. We had been counting on making extra money on the dinners to cover expenses, but we'd figure other ways to compensate. I knew there would be challenges, so we just kept moving ahead.

We faced a possible glitch in the Governor's schedule when his political advisors planned to take the Secretary of Agriculture to another meeting in the Governor's helicopter. We didn't want that to happen, obviously, so with our Congressman Ned Patterson's help, we got the helicopter to forego the nearby landing site of the other meeting because of "safety" concerns, and instead directed it to land where we wanted it to. A few minutes later all eyes turned as a formation of half a dozen State Police cars flashed and blared their way to the center of town. The Governor made a grand entrance, indeed.

The main program included discussions about milk marketing by professors from Cornell University and the University of Connecticut along with Joel Blum who headed the Federal Milk Marketing Orders. Farmers were thinking of ways to produce more but they weren't focused on how to sell more, and I wanted to change that if I could.

Just bringing key officials and businessmen together with the farmers would go a long way toward making changes. I hoped it would be a chance for people like Bud Fischer, the initiator of bulk milk services on the east coast, to influence the decision-makers who ran state government. The governor of Connecticut sent a representative who attended the event along with other dignitaries including Congressman Patterson and state legislative leader Larry Lane. A big reception was catered under a colorful yellow and white striped tent in front of Mom and Dad's 300-year-old farmhouse. Contributors to Dairy Day including a Wisconsin builder of bulk milk trucks were feted. Secretary of Agriculture Burgland had already presented Fischer with a plaque honoring his contributions to bulk milk services in the whole region, and since our farm was one of the pioneering farms on his first route, I took vicarious pleasure in the honor.

Everything was not official, however. Among the humorous anecdotes of the day, I enjoyed the high jinx of one lovely regional character meeting the distinguished Governor of the State of New York.

THE GOVERNOR
PREFERS HOME COOKING

Brad Peck was a life long friend of Dad's, and along with his second wife, Ellie, he was a contributor to the events of the day. They lived in nearby Egermont, Massachusetts, where Ellie maintained a blissful ignorance of New York State politics. Ellie Peck was rather tall and elegant, the kind of woman you'd want at a cocktail fundraiser to impress the honored guests and potential donors. She had lived her whole life in Massachusetts before coming to Copake as Brad Peck's second wife. She knew little about New York State politics and politicians. Governor Carey and Agriculture Secretary Burgland were strangers to her. She happened to be hard of hearing, and as luck would have it, she was destined to meet the governor.

Governor Carey figured to make some political hay with his helicopter visit to Dairy Day. The event promised to boost the reputations of the local sponsors too, so the Governor was primed to plunge into the crowd to shake hands and exchange hearty greetings. It was no surprise that his taste for stylish women caught up with Ellie. Sporting flashy jewelry and holding a tall glass of iced libations, she attracted the attention of the governor's aides, and in no time one of the aides stepped up to the worldly looking Ellie Peck and said, "I would like you to meet the Governor of the State of New York, Hue Carey"

Ellie, not facing the aid and too vain to wear a hearing aid, hadn't heard a word. She turned to the Governor. She said, "Oh, do you live around here?" Ellie didn't recognize the governor at all.

Governor Carey was surprised but managed an upbeat reference to Albany, and the Executive Mansion where he lived with his family. Ellie nodded attentively without understanding a word of what the governor said.

"Do you farm, too?" she asked. With that, the governor was whisked away in search of a more impressionable prospect.

The Governor felt more at home in the kitchen where he chatted with my mother and the caterers. The three of them called themselves "The High Bonnets," and when Governor Carey discovered that one of them had nine children, genuine conversation broke out about large families. He had 14 children himself, and talking about life in child-dominated households may have been the high point of the day for the governor.

Everything else was milk, money and politics, not to mention good old self-promotion. Secretary Burgland posed for pictures with the farmers and was interested in what we thought, but I was disappointed by the small number of COOP leaders who were there to make the case for equitable pricing for farmers of the Northeast. The cost of producing milk here was higher than in the Midwest, but hauling costs were higher too. That is because of the greater distances milk is hauled to city milk plants. By federal order, the farmer had to pay for hauling. The Northeast still has a need for recognition, education and lobbying in order to compete with other dairy producing regions. The Milk Industry Foundation, a processor organization, is out there lobbying for lower prices too.

Because of my leadership in organizing the 1978 Dairy Day, I learned it is possible for one person to change the system. I had the platform I needed to propose a priority lien law at a Farm Bureau meeting. In milk marketing, the processors collected the farmers' milk, processed it, and sent it to the stores. Then after the store sells the milk, he collects the money from the stores. The money is put in a bank account called the receivables. After the government calculates the price, and on a date specified by law, the farmer is paid for the milk he shipped the month before. If processors are falling behind with secured loans or a banks decided not to renew an old loan, the bank would call the loans and seizing the receivables the day before the farmers have to be paid. It was costing farmers tens of millions of dollars in some instances. Because of my resolution, the bonding of processors was required in New York. Wisconsin passed similar legislation. It was definitely a peak accomplishment in my life.

MY BIG BARN FALLS TO FIRE: AUGUST 24, 1985

Frank was feeling pleased with himself after finishing the milking all by himself. It was a beautiful summer evening and he thought he would go up on the hill, check on the crops and take in the magnificent view of the mountains across the valley before he ate. Up on top he got curious to see what progress had been made on the house Ben Ackley's son in law was building. He was out of sight of the barn when he heard the fire siren, then he saw smoke coming from the direction the barn was. He was devastated when he came over the brow of the hill and saw flames shooting high above the barn. It was the first time he did the milking all by himself. Now the future of the farm was in doubt.

The Duchess County Fair has one of the best cattle shows in the state. I was probably still waiting in line to get into the fair when Frank was coming down off the hill. The first thing I did when I got to the fair was look up Don Briggs. He was in the new cattle barn. After I visited with him a bit I went out to see the rest of the fair. I remember walking down from the main gate past the building where the old cattle barn was. I remember staying with the cattle there when Dad was showing Weber Burk Clover Lad. Clover Lad usually took home the grand champion ribbon. The fair was much smaller back then. When I got back to the cattle barn about 9, I was given the news that my big barn had burned. The fire was discovered just before seven. It seemed that by the time I got back there would be little to save. The trip back from Rhinebeck seemed long. How would I care for the cows?

The driveway had fire hoses strung everywhere. Water was still being pumped through main lines along the road and fire trucks were everywhere. While some still hosed down the hay other firemen were picking up the fire hose; their job was done. The front of the old McGee barn, where the farm office and milk house stood in defiance of the destruction around it, the name Langdonhurst still showed at the top. The cement block main barn with its tall arched roof was gone. In its place was a huge mound of smoldering hay. I walked past the office to where the milking parlor was just a mass of burned timbers, tin and destroyed equipment. When I got back to where the six silos stood only the second floor grain room remained and complete destruction all around. My new aluminum extension ladder melted off at the top, with the bottom still shinny and bright. Further back was the untouched free stall barn, now useless with no water and no electricity. Standing in front of the barn was my foreman, Mr. Bradway, with Frank, Bob and Mike and Dad. Mr. Bradway had things set up to take the cattle to Bull Spring Farm. Char Peck, the owner, had already been contacted. The rent would be $650 a month. I took one look around and gave my nod. The cattle were loaded and Mr. Bradway and the boys took charge of the cattle. Then I walked around and looked at the devastation. The entire second cutting was made but there was still a third to be made, But where to put it? What about the corn crop?

What I saw was devastating. It would take weeks to be able to get feed from the silos. That would take electricity. There was no way to get water to the remaining barns and the house. Production was going to plummet. All the cows in the late stage of lactation would stand dry for a long time. It would take a full year before production would return. Around back I saw Henry Call, the fire investigator for the fire company. "Where did it start?" I asked. He said, "The only smoke was coming from back by the silos when it was first seen." Then it moved to the main barn and everything was on fire.

If that wasn't bad enough, the investigation he did the next day raised more questions than it answered. He and the fire chief, Dell Walton, were waiting for the state investigators to help determine why the fire had moved from the back of the barn to the front of the barn. The state people failed to arrive and the local fire company officials eventually went home. It then seemed to me that the state people believed the fire was caused by arson. However, without the state investigators and their equipment, it couldn't be determined.

The absence of the authoritative and more expert state investigators may have let the local officials say the cause was probably electrical in nature. According to reports in the newspaper, Call had established the cause of the fire as faulty wiring in the calf room at the back of the barn. My son Cliff had taken pictures of the fire scene that directly refuted Call's assessment of the fire's origin. Cliff's photos showed some fire above the calf room, but the front of the barn was fully engulfed in flame. Call was somewhat taken back by the photos and decided to carry a camera with him on subsequent fire investigations.

The rest of the summer seemed to be taken up with a string of fires including a horse barn torched in August and a storage barn across the street from the lumberyard. That fire was stopped in time to save the building.

TROUBLE SMOKES THE HORIZON

An earlier fire that really comes back to me as particularly tragic hit the George Partridge place July 14, 1982. It stands out as an example of how fire destroys hopes, dreams and hard work, eroding the underpinnings of a farmer's life.

I was awakened by the fire siren around half past midnight, and stood on the porch looking at the red glow in the sky to the north before heading out to join the traffic going by Brown's Dam and Bull Spring Farm. I thought about George. He didn't seem to have an enemy in the world and he worked hard to achieve the ultimate goal of owning his own farm. He had milked cows for other farmers, driven the school bus and worked as a hired hand for many other farmers in the area. The fire was a blow he would not be able to overcome.

George had built up a nice herd, but the morning after the fire, he had 57 cows and seven calves to bury. Insurance paid around $600 in replacement costs per head, but as he learned through painful experience at auction a few months later, it wouldn't be enough to rebuild his business. I sat near him at the Chatham fairgrounds as an auction for replacement stock took place. My heart sank as I watched George and his family sit helplessly, not able to bid on the cows that passed by. Each one drew bids in the neighborhood of $1,300. George would have to sell his farm, and eventually, a New York City investor purchased it.

In October that same year, Buel Peck's horse barn, which bordered my pasture, caught fire. The sheriff left it under investigation. How I reacted personally may be a clue as to how others in the community responded to the fires all around. I kept on working myself to the point of exhaustion so that by the time the big barn at Jensen's caught fire in August of 1984, I slept through the commotion. The next morning I drove down to Jensen's and found my old friends, Pete and Mary Lou Jensen standing with family at the end of their driveway. They were very upset with me that I hadn't attended the fire during the night. It was painful to explain how I had slept through the siren, which was next to my house. An investigation of the fire turned up a report of a man seen running along the brook. A matchbook was also found, but nothing else. Bull Call, the fire company's fire investigator, had been sent to New York to study arson detection. It didn't seem to help him or the fire company or the sheriff in any efforts to stop the Copake fires.

I became acutely aware of the potential danger to the Brown barn. It was close to the road and no houses were nearby. My grandfather swapped land along the lake to get the barn after Mr. Brown died in the 1930s. Brown had made his money in the city and moved up to what used to be the Unity Gristmill in 1910. He demolished the mill where farmers ground their grain as far back as the Revolution. Then he replaced the old dam with a bigger concrete dam that flooded the land of adjacent property owners. After a successful legal defense of those actions, he built a Tudor mansion and moved out of the mill house where he had spent his first days in Copake. Brown also built a big two-story barn, fitted out much like a fortress with iron bars over the basement windows and heavy sliding doors made of weathered cypress. He kept his Pierce Arrow in the basement. The barn, of course, was a cherished asset and I worried about it constantly. I had much of my equipment stored there in the off season.

My own losses by fire were suffered in a nightmarish cycle of fires that took in friends and neighbors from the entire area. But Copake seemed to be the center of the activity, and it proceeded for years, so long, in fact, that The Independent, the area's primary newspaper, published a ten year retrospective of the fires with names, dates and locations (see entire listing at end of book). The article noted that the hub of the frequent fires was Copake. Many of the fires were suspected arsons, but few were linked with actual arsonists.

Ten years of blazes encompassed some 50 fires counting back from the Copake Movie Theatre near the center of the village in June 1990, to the Pine Plains Lumber Company, on County Route 7 in Gallatin, in 1980. It's hard to believe that that many fires could happen in any one such circumscribed area, unless the fires were intentionally set. One man, Eugene Shackleton of Hillsdale was convicted of burglary and arson in a VFW Hall fire in 1983. Another arsonist, Lawrence W. Conklin Jr., pleaded guilty to an arson fire and was convicted in 1987, but the fires did not stop. Over the course of the decade, all kinds of fires erupted. Cars, mobile homes, a pickup or two, big farm machines, barns and houses all suited the taste of the fire monger. I had to start over after two of those fires hit my dairy business, but it did not blind me to the vulnerability of other members of the Copake community or turn me against my neighbors in suspicion or vengeance. I was in sync with law enforcement at the time, too. Advertising and funding for a reward leading to the apprehension of the arsonist was my own major public initiative, and I pursued it through the press and my own personal contacts.

After my second fire I was forced to rent Bull Spring Farm to manage my dairy operation. This was when my attitude changed, and I began to directly confront law enforcement officials. The sheriff's department seemed to be glossing over the problem saying the cause was electrical, unknown and so forth. I was told not to say anything about arson or the insurance company wouldn't pay, as if I would have to sue to get the money. Why were we tolerating the devastating attacks on our property and livelihoods as if insurance money were somehow the antidote to having your life go up in smoke? It didn't work for me. The law, as enforced by the sheriff (Proper), seemed as if it was more beneficial to ignore or cover-up information leading to the arrest of the arsonist than to fully and openly investigate the fires.

DIVERSITY: COULD THE FARM BUSINESS BE SAVED?

Farming in general was a struggling business, especially with dairy in the northeast. One night, I came across an ad for a seminar scheduled for Des Moines, Iowa. The main focus would be on new enterprises begun by farmers to diversify their businesses. It didn't take Frank and I long to decide to give it a try. Once there, we rented a room and visited with farmers from all over the country. During the convention, small group discussions got us thinking about all kinds of options, and on the way home we realized that although we didn't have a clear vision, we certainly had gotten a broad view of what could be done.

Our next trip to Knoxville, Tennessee was different. We went with the specific purpose in mind to check out Honey Acre greenhouse. The hydroponics greenhouse was designed to specialize in growing tomatoes, and the manufacturers were trying to develop brand name recognition for it. Eventually we set one up in Copake. The tomatoes tasted great, but I was disappointed with the level of production. One of our suppliers stopped by on his rounds and noticed the greenhouse operation with great enthusiasm. He said we would have no problem selling plants from the same operation, so I bought a selection of plants in mid-February and found that geraniums grew very well in the bottom heat of the Honey Acre system. When the seed supplier returned in April, there were so many plants that he advised me to line up a place to sell them. He didn't think I could possibly market enough of them through the greenhouse location, but things turned out okay. When the weather broke, people turned out and the plants sold so well that I decided to double the plantings for the next year.

The opportunity to subdivide and sell some of my farmland was a lot more complicated, and it didn't turn out nearly as well as the greenhouse. My realtor friend called to negotiate a deal for a customer who wanted to build a small apartment complex. He needed land, of course, and I had a big flat to the east side of town that was zoned for the appropriate use. At $6,000 for 20 acres, the potential was there to bolster the farm business in a major way.

The land at the end of Taconic Street extended to Mountain View Road and a new road opening the land for development seemed like it would be good for the town. There would be a cluster development near Mountain View Road but most of the rest of the 20 acres would be open space. I wasted no time getting to the real estate office to sign papers and to put money in escrow. The developer would build the road from Taconic Street to Mountain View road. I hired the surveyor and my lawyer guided me through the process of getting the subdivision. It looked like a dream come true.

About this time I was looking across Church Street at the empty lot where my barn had stood. Sheriff Proper drove by and parked his car. He came over to my yard and expressed his sympathy for my fire loss. He suggested I put up a Dairy Queen. I was grateful for the idea, but I didn't particularly want to build a Dairy Queen. Then the conversation shifted to the subject of the arson fires.

The sheriff said he had a suspect for one of the fires; the person had failed a lie detector test, but a second piece of evidence was required to make an arrest, and the suspect was released because of the lack of corroborating evidence. The sheriff confided that the suspect was a fireman and that the fire company had sent him to arson school. Then the sheriff got specific by saying he had a suspect for the George Partridge fire who had worked for Partridge. That ended that conversation. He broke off in mid sentence and then changed the subject. It was as if he realized he just said too much. This chance meeting came to mind many times over the course of the coming events. It meant that the sheriff knew the Partridge fire was arson all along. It was not an electrical fire like he told the papers. Dairy Queens and arsonists made a strange combination of things for me to worry about, but I had a pretty good idea who had worked for George Partridge.

As I should have suspected by this time, the subdivision of my land for a tidy business profit was an opportunity that melted away in the circumstances of the times. A public hearing had to be held on the proposal, and a signed petition opposing the subdivision had circulated among the neighbors and most of them were there to present it to the town board. Even though the zoning regulations were met by the proposal, I could see that the town supervisor was not about to anger the opposition.

I remember the testimony of Martha Wilson best. She dashed to the supervisor's table and pounded out her message with her fist. "They will ruin the water I drink; I won't be able to drink my water!" This is the same retired, two-room schoolhouse teacher who lived in a house on Taconic Street and transported her drinking water from a well on the property of a house she still owned in Taghkanic. I was surprised at her out-of-order performance.

The clincher came from the highway superintendent who demanded a wider turn at Taconic Street. I would have to call in the surveyor again and present new maps. Suddenly, the sale was on the slow track, if it was on track at all. The town's response sent a clear message of non-support for my efforts to recover from the fire. It certainly showed me that the community spirit of my father's times had changed. People turned inward, looking at their own property concerns with calloused attitudes. I was simply a neighbor, so to speak. I decided to let the surveyor handle the next hearing on the subdivision. It was suggested that if the sale failed each of the people that signed the petition could be sued. The development had met the community development plan and the zoning requirements, but I preferred not to sue.

STRUCTURE FIRE AT BULL SPRING FARM: COPAKE FIRE DEPARTMENT SCANNER, JUNE 15, 1987

The dramatic events and recollections of a fire are set against a backdrop of mundane routine. It was still light on the June 15 evening of the big blaze at Bull Spring Farm. Frank and I were poking about the kitchen in the business of getting some supper. Frank was pan-frying hamburger for himself. He had come home late because he'd stopped to visit his friend and fellow farmer, Ernie, just down the road a little. After milking and checking dry cows, he wasn't in much of a hurry. I had been waiting for him to eat, but went ahead and ate and returned the hamburger and potato salad to the refrigerator. When Frank showed up he was fending for himself and had just started cooking his hamburger when the fire alert wailed on his scanner. Frank abandoned the stove and headed for the door. As a fairly new volunteer, he didn't want to be late to the fire. I just turned off the stove, then the fire alert sounded again, and I moved closer to the scanner to hear the report.

"Structure fire at Bull Spring Farm."

I ran upstairs for my shoes and hurried out to the car. Anger and panic flushed my face. From the speeding car it wasn't long before I spotted flames shooting 40 feet above the barn roof. The fire chief was setting up the reserve tank and more fire trucks and firemen arrived. I parked along the road just past Lilly's house and jumped over the fence to get across the pasture to the barn. The crackling fire pressed in on my eardrums in a sound I'll never forget.

It was my third fire, and I didn't give a shit what the sheriff or anyone else said about not mentioning arson! I vowed to raise hell. After having three barns burned I had a right to be mad.

Getting the calves out took a heroic effort, but the chaos and noise didn't deter me from demanding an investigation. In fact I made quit a bit of noise about it. There was no way the fires of Copake could all be accidental, especially not this one.

I demanded an arson investigation, saw the owner and had him sign a request with the sheriff. It wasn't long until the press showed up, including all three local TV news channels. I remember one reporter asking if I thought someone was out to get me. I told him he was out to get me, but not just me. We had an arsonist. He was burning a lot of business. We had a big problem. I knew this was the last thing Sheriff Proper wanted the press to hear, but I had had enough.

Given what I told the press it didn't surprise me when Sheriff Proper came to me and asked if Frank would take a lie detector test at the sheriff's office. Given that I was the one demanding an investigation I could hardly say no. I asked Frank and he agreed as long as I went along. It was set up for that Friday. A deputy would pick us up.

It was going to be a long night. We had to find a place to milk the cows in a few hours. All my men were there helping. We checked out several farms, but in each case there was a problem. We weren't able locate another barn to move the cows to. The last chance seemed to be the Jenkins farm, but I had to wait for a return call for an answer. I sent the men home to try to get some rest and I went back to the house to wait for the phone call. I would call and let the men know how I did. Other than that we had no backup plan. Soon there was a knock on the door. When I answered it, it was Investigator Shook and Deputies Kane and Wilson. Investigator Shook said he wanted to go over what happened with each of us, but one at a time and in private. I let them use my office. They took Frank in first and said they would talk to my son Cliff and I after. When they came out they said the learned everything they needed from Frank and they didn't have to question the rest of us.

I was seated on the couch when Investigator Shook asked me if I had a suspect. I told him yes. Then I named the man I believed had worked for George Partridge whom Sheriff Proper had named as a suspect in that fire. The man I named also fit the bill of being a fireman and having been sent to arson school. Shook's fists tightened and he raised them and thrust them down three times while he repeated the man's name and turned in a complete counter-clockwise circle in front of me. I was amazed at his reaction. After he regained his composure, I told him more. One of the things I told him was that I had seen him driving slowly down the street about a month before, apparently eyeing my free stall barn. I was standing out in front of the greenhouse at the time. It upset me so much I call the insurance company to check my coverage and discussed the matter with my neighbor. My neighbor was suspicious of him too, but for other reasons. It was well past two when I finally got the call and confirmed that I had a barn for the cows. I called the men.

CURSED?

I was haunted by the cruel coincidence of a third barn fire. No! It was not a coincidence; the fire had been deliberately set! That night I had no idea how the fire was set. I looked at all the open fields, the Lilly family on one side and Fran Dick by the driveway, and saw no way for an arsonist to get in and then out without being seen. That is what I told the Independent. I knew where the fire started, but I did not know how.

What's interesting to me is how things slow down in recollection, and it's possible to carefully rerun scenes in your mind so that you can see something you missed before. About a year after the fire, for instance, I was watching TV when they showed a picture of a man running backward trying to set some kind of record or something. I recognized the movements the man was making. They were the same movements as the person in my pasture the night of the fire; movement that hadn't occurred to me when I first saw the man now made sense. The man hadn't been going out in the pasture to get a better view; he was running backward while watching the fire. It was then that the recollection of a man near the Bull Spring fire scene gave me the missing picture of evidence in my story of the fire. I had seen the man who burned my barn!

MY GRANDFATHER WAS A HORSEMAN

A.D. worked with horses his whole life, and his knowledge of horses was widely respected. Henry Folger owned the auction barn at the end of Main Street. He had a few horses that he worked out at Ben Ackley's Empire Farm.

A.D. stopped down at Ben's track one day as Henry was unloading a new horse he had bought in Saratoga. While Ben and Henry admired the horse, they asked A.D. what he thought. A.D. wanted to see the horse walk around a bit, and the horse appeared to be in excellent shape, silky coat and all. A.D. stepped around in front of the horse, took hold of his halter and looked him over very closely.

"What do you think," Henry asked, proudly.

"Well, Henry, I'm sorry, but he doesn't look so good." They exchanged dumfounded looks. "What do you mean?" Henry asked.

A.D. repeated himself as he got back into his car and drove away. A few days later he returned to Ben's track and learned that Henry had gotten rid of the horse. It turned out the horse was blind.

FALSE AND MALICIOUS ARREST GUARANTEES FREEDOM FOR THE GUILTY

> I am bound on a wheel of fire that mine own tears do scald like molten lead.
>
> —Shakespeare: King Lear

My day started out great. I had a lead on a contractor for the new barn. I went to Langdon Curtis' place to talk about building the milk house and the flat barn. We didn't have any trouble agreeing on the cost and work schedule. Driving home, I felt more upbeat than I had at any time since the Bull Spring barn had burned. Frank's idea of implementing a California flat barn instead of using a regular milking parlor was working out, so while he ran the dairy, I could run the greenhouse, and together, the operations would begin to make money again. My mood fit the bright, sunny day perfectly.

Back home, I poured myself a cup of coffee and simply enjoyed feeling good. Then, the sheriff's Bronco pulled up at the vegetable stand out front. I went out to see what was going on. Frank stood quietly while one of the two deputies, David Proper, did the talking. He said that Frank had spoken with them the day before about a clerk at Stewart's who had sold him beer, illegally, of course.

"We are after this clerk, see and we want Frank to identify her," David said.

He assured me that Frank wouldn't get into any trouble; all they wanted him to do was walk into the store and identify the clerk. They weren't going to do anything to Frank. "We will go straight in and straight back," David Proper promised. "It will only take a short time. We won't take him any place else. Just straight out and right back"

I looked in the back seat of the Bronco where Charlie Wilson was sitting. It looked odd, Charlie was grinning from ear to ear. He was a teacher in Frank's Sunday school and he and David, the sheriff's son, were on the fire company together with Frank, so even though I was reluctant to agree with the plan, which would mean I'd have to tend the stand and maybe delay a neces-

sary trip to Millerton, I finally accepted based on a prompt return. Charlie pushed the seat forward, got out and loaded Frank
in the back. Then he flipped the seat back and got in front.

It was noon when I gave up waiting for Frank, closed the
stand and left for Millerton. I returned around 2:30, and still, no
Frank. I unloaded supplies at the greenhouse and walked across
the road toward the closed vegetable stand. Ethel Stang was on
her porch and called out to me.

"It wasn't right for them to take Frank like that. What they
did was wrong." She went back to her chair, and when I got back
to my house, I began to worry. I put in a call to the sheriff's office
and got the secretary who put me on hold until Sheriff Proper
came on the line.

"Frank has something to tell you," Sheriff Proper said.
"Here he is." Then I heard him talk to Frank in the background.
"Tell him, Frank; tell your father what you did." He repeated
it several times. Then after a long silence Frank finally said,
"Hi, Dad."

The sounds of my son's distressed voice alarmed me. The
sheriff kept urging Frank to talk to me, then, he simply told me
that Frank had burned my big barn and burned Bull Spring, too.
"He signed a confession." I literally fell into my chair.

I mustered the breath to ask if Frank would be arrested, and
Sheriff Proper said he had to, but that he would see what he
could do. All I knew was that Frank needed help, and after I got
off the phone to the sheriff's office, I called my lawyer Tom Griffin where I got the usual delaying response from the secretary before he returned my stressful call. I demanded that something be
done. Griffin cut the call short so he could call the sheriff's office
to stop the questioning of Frank immediately. While I was caught
up in the calls to Griffin, my brother popped in. He'd already
heard from the sheriff about Frank's confession and he wanted
to know if I was all right. It was a real rarity for him to stop by
to see me, and when I told him I was waiting for a return call
from Tom Griffin, he just said, "I guess you're okay," and left.
Amazing. Not a quarter of an hour later, Langdon Curtis stopped
by, pounding on my door. He stepped off the porch as I opened
the door.

"You'll have to find somebody else to build your barn; I'm
not going to do it. I didn't know about Frank this morning. Sorry

to hear about it." He headed back to his truck by the roadside and I went back inside to the desk where I sat and wondered how word got out so fast. Then, Griffin called again. The arraignment was scheduled in Copake court before Judge Kane. Griffin arranged bail for $1,000, and I had an hour to pull the money together. That was a real trick because the bank was closed. I asked to see a copy of the confession, but it wasn't going to be ready until the next day. The scramble was on, but I managed to raise enough cash for bail.

Judge Kane sat at the head of the courtroom, and as people meandered in, they looked at me and took seats on the opposite side of the room. When Sheriff Proper came in he approached me to say that Frank was scared that I wouldn't stick by him. "You have to let him know you will be there for him," Proper said. The sudden rush of events still burned in my mind and I kept hearing the words "he confessed" hiss in my ears.

What followed couldn't be helped apparently, but it was Copake's version of big-time news, complete with Frank being lead through the side door in handcuffs in front of the gathering crowd of locals. The press, forewarned by the sheriff, was poised by the door for pictures. Frank tried to shield his face from the photographers as he bowed his head. Two deputies, including David Proper, sandwiched Frank like he was a prize. Once inside the courtroom, they removed the cuffs. The arraignment was over soon enough, even though it felt like forever. I paid the $1,000 cash bail, and Frank and I left by the side door. He was too stressed to talk.

The arrest took place just a week after a story in the *New York Times* appeared. It was the July 13, 1987 issue and the story was titled; *Rural New York, a time of Ferment.* The story opened with an interview of me citing the problem created by the three barn fires and the problem in the community. The reporter also tried to interview Sheriff Proper. When he asked the sheriff if the primary suspect is a local volunteer firefighter who was questioned by the Columbia County Sheriff and who failed a polygraph test, the sheriff would not comment. The sheriff added, "Everybody knows everybody. That's what you are up against in a small town."

Early the next morning, the phone rang and I sat at the desk to answer it. Murray Jenkins said he'd just heard about Frank.

He was sorry, and he wanted to know what had happened. I had to say I really wasn't sure. Then his wife Barbara got on the phone. She was very religious, so I wasn't surprised when she told me to take the Lord's hand and walk through the valleys and across the hills. Then she said, "You must get out of our barn." That killed conversation pretty quick. And, any notion I might have had about taking the Lord's hand turned to worries about a new contractor and how I would face the specter of managing lawyers as well as cows.

There was nothing to do but stumble forward. Griffin showed up around 11 with a new lawyer, Jason Shaw, who had experience as an Assistant DA in New York City. He knew arson cases and he brought the copy of Frank's confession. It didn't take me long to pick the thing apart. First, Frank's handwriting was obviously not the one making out the script. As I learned, however, it was standard operating procedure for the actual confessions to be written out by the police or the interrogators and then signed by the accused. Second, it claimed that a cigarette had been flicked into a hay mound to start the fire, but Frank did not smoke, and third, no farm boy would ever come up with the term "hay mound" for haymow. Of course, Frank had not phrased the confession in the first place. I still doubt whether Frank grasped the significance of the meaning of what he signed. For me, the whole confession raised a series of improbable facts. It was an outright fabrication, and my anger began to overwhelm my sense of logic. Where did Frank get a cigarette? The way his truck was described as parked, Frank would have had to drive a short distance, stop, and walk around the front of his truck before "flicking" the cigarette through a door that was at least 12 feet above ground. If anyone really wanted to burn the barn why wouldn't he use a match to make sure he got the job done? It didn't make sense, and it didn't sound like the way Frank would do anything, whether he started the fire or not. Griffin and I talked about defending Frank, and I was convinced that the new lawyer was best qualified to take the case at $100 an hour.

Frank's trusting nature had served him poorly, and I agonized over how to proceed as I listened to his story about how things happened that day on the ride to nowhere. Frank considered David Proper, the sheriff's son and deputy, a good friend. He and Frank had gone out to lunch a number of times together so, Frank trusted him. David had even served Frank beer one time after they returned from a fire.

That made it easy for Frank to volunteer to aid his friend in an investigation involving both the sheriff's department and him. The case involved a problem with underage drinking, and Frank was apparently involved as the underage purchaser of a six-pack of beer. The day before the arrest Frank agreed to go along. They proceeded to the police station at the town hall, but instead of bringing Frank back home as they had promised, they took him on a ride along a deserted road near Hillsdale and grilled him about the fire. Frank repeated his movements and whereabouts from the evening of the fire to no avail. He was accused of starting the fire.

According to the two deputies, the girl in question was not working at the store when they went. Frank said he was taken right to the sheriff's office in Hudson and didn't even stop at the store. At the sheriff's office, a skillful team consisting of John Morgan from the New York State Office of Fire Prevention and Control and Investigator Cozzolino interrogated him. Sheriff Proper sent his son, David Proper, to get lunch from the county jail for Frank. Then David was sent out on patrol.

Morgan and Cozzolino took turns interrogation Frank. Cozzolino pounded the table, demanding Frank tell him the truth about what happened, even though Frank did his best to repeat the details of his movements and whereabouts. "That's not what happened," Morgan shouted as Frank recounted his milking chores and the visit with a friend named Ernie. Interrogators rotated and the line of questioning was repeated. Frank was apparently worn down and intimidated, and since he didn't know, and therefore exercise, his rights of representation, he grew increasingly fearful and isolated.

"Be a fucking man! Admit you did it! Own up to it!" As it turned out, Cozzolino wrote the statement. It figured that phrases like "hay mound" came from his ignorance of farming.

When David returned, he did not take Frank home as Frank wanted. He was sent in to talk with Frank. He was the good cop. He tried to get Frank to sign the statement, and he continued the questioning. At that point it must have seemed hopeless to Frank. "Start a new day," David urged. Frank finally relented and signed as his good friend advised. To this day, I wish he hadn't given in, but we can't change that now, or ever.

As I learned later, a second piece of corroborating evidence was needed to support the confession. Frank told me he had given a ride to the fire truck driver, Bob, the night of the fire, because Bob had flagged him down for a ride. Frank asked where the fire was and Bob had apparently called in to learn where to go. Bob said it was at Bull Spring. They rounded the corner and the smoke clearly showed the way to Bull Spring Farm. Bob later gave a statement saying Frank had driven straight to the fire as if he knew where it was. I asked Frank myself what had happened, and he said that Bob had told him where the fire was: Bull Spring. Besides, Frank could see the smoke from town, so he let Bob out and drove to the fire. He went directly into the house there, to call me.

It was obvious to me that Frank was not the arsonist. It didn't make sense in any way or form that you might look at the possibility. His personal devotion to the animals and the farm itself in addition to the reconstructed facts of the fire eliminated Frank as a suspect. Knowing Frank as I have, for his whole life, I am incapable of believing in anything but his innocence. It's really the key element in this whole story.

FRANK AND THE DEMOLAY

Frank Langdon, my son, was a happy kid. The first time I saw him at the hospital he had a smile on his face. He always greeted you with cheer and a big smile. Even as a little guy he seemed to project a joy about where he was in the moment. When he started school he had speech impediment but a little help from a therapist took care of that. It didn't seem to affect his self-confidence. Frank wanted to please people, and he compensated for not being particularly quick with words by being quick with friendship and trust, which ingratiated him to many people.

Frank was always industrious and helpful around the farm and he loved animals too, which inspired him along the way, in growing up and in raising and showing prize-winning Holsteins at the county fairs and competitions. He was looking forward to taking over the farm someday from the very start.

When he was a kid, Frank sold sweet corn from a little roadside stand, and he always treated the customers with deference. If they picked up an ear of corn and slit it lengthwise with a fingernail to get a look at the ripeness of the kernels, Frank would just take that ear and drop it in the trash, giving the customer another to replace it. His brother Cliff would never make a problem with customers either, but he'd be torn up inside over something like that and turn away in frustration. Frank simply took it as part of the business.

When the corn was ready for sale, competing stands charged high prices for the first corn, then as the season progressed and supply increased, they'd lower the price of corn. Not Frank. He was honest and fair. He started out at ten cents an ear and charged the same rate all summer. Customers that stopped early in the season liked that consistency in price, and kept coming back. They also liked the way Frank called them by name every time they stopped by. I remember the day the road was under repair and traffic was diverted, but Frank stayed out there just the same to serve a few of his customers. He'd stand out there all day to make $15. For Frank it was all part of the business, and he liked doing it.

Frank's sincerity and his ambition to become a leader in his field made his acceptance into the DeMolay International seem like a natural and logical course to follow. He was enthusiastic and active. His consistent efforts at organization and leadership guided the local chapter to high levels of success with events like ski trips and village-centered get-togethers. Frank's involvement in the DeMolay organization made the criminal charges of arson, and his subsequent arrest, a total contradiction of everything he was and had become.

"The namesake of the Order of DeMolay was born in Vitrey, Department of Haute Saone, France in 1244" (DeMolay International Website). When he was 21, Jacques DeMolay became a member of the Order of the Knights Templar, an organization sanctioned by the Roman Catholic Church in 1128. The knights guarded the road between Jerusalem and Acre, and they were known for acts of heroism and valor from their participation in the Crusades. The attraction of the Order for nobles and princes made it wealthy, and the envy of authoritative leaders like Philip the Fair, King of France. In fact, they were jealous of the group's power and status.

In 1305, Philip the Fair began to act against the Knights Templars' exclusive accountability to the Church. Within two years, persecution of the Knights was underway and Jacques DeMolay was taken prisoner along with hundreds of others and cast into a dungeon. In the meantime, Philip manipulated Pope Clement into condemning the Templars, giving Philip the freedom to confiscate their property and their wealth.

DeMolay, Grand Master of the Templars, became a target for interrogation and torture, but he refused to reveal the location of the Order's funds. He also refused to betray any of his comrades. DeMolay was tried in a special court on March 18, 1314. He was presented with a forged confession as evidence against him, but he disavowed the confession, a crime punishable by death. For his loyalty and valor, DeMolay was burned at the stake along with a fellow Knight, Guy of Auvergne.

I don't think anyone expected Frank to carry on a twelfth-century tradition. I doubt most people around Copake ever heard the full story, but the DeMolay connection to the Masons was well-known, and the progression from one organization to the other was commonly assumed to be the course of promotion for upstanding young men of the DeMolay. Standing up for the truth in the face of temptations of safe passage and even temporal power was a hallmark of DeMolay. For me, it was then and is now a characteristic of my son, Frank. When he was presented with a false confession and forced to sign it, the comparison to the situation of the young DeMolay of so many years ago was painful indeed. I suffered the shame and shunning right along with Frank.

I cringed, when I heard the cries of "firebug" and "the torch" ring out across the village square. These people were referring to my son. One night when he went bowling a group of young men gathered in a circle with their arms around each other and chanted, "Barn Burner, Barn Burner, Barn Burner." He was being shunned. In my heart, I knew that the suspicion would not be completely thwarted even when the truth came out. It was clear, Copake wanted to target someone. They wanted to put a face on the arsonist. The real arsonist was still out there setting fires. He must have been only too glad to see the village choose my son. Although the charges were dropped in an odd manner you will find out about later in the book, it didn't seem to matter. I didn't occur to the citizens of Copake, that the problem was unsolved, that the arsonist (or arsonists) was still on the loose.

In retrospect, it all makes a certain amount of sense, but at the time as events unfolded, I couldn't get on top of the situations. Worried about building a new barn, and the demands of feeding and milking cows on a daily basis, I got blind sided by the arrest of my son. I was also caught up in the sudden need for cash and I got mixed messages from the community and especially, my family and close friends. It was as if Frank and I carried a plague: we were pariahs, firebugs. Few in the community knew that Frank worked as hard as he did for the farm, or even that we had agreed on a partnership when he got out of college. Perhaps there was a bit of jealousy with some people too. When the community decided to zone the main parcel it was zoned as residential, which made it very valuable.

A WEB OF FINANCIAL
SETBACKS FOLLOWS THE ARREST

I should point out that the Bull Spring fire put extra pressure on my already tenuous business situation. I had sold 20 acres of my land for $120,000 before the fire, but the buyer withdrew because of public opposition and my emerging legal troubles that would unfold later. A lower price was offered but my lawyer at the time advised me not to sell at that price. He said as a subdivision it would always be worth much more. The 20 acres was part of a larger parcel that I turned down a million dollars for not long before. Frank and I talked it over and he said he wanted to keep farming and the money problem wasn't pressing at the time. Now I needed money. I needed $35,000 to rebuild the milk house and flat barn. We were also trying to expand the new greenhouse business, and with no prospect of profit, an opportunity to move two houses onto the Copake farm property for speculation looked good to me. The savings bank wanted to expand and put the houses up for sale. It turned out it was too good to be truly that simple. A neighbor disputed property lines and sewerage systems to the tune of an extra $16,000, and a variety of holdups contributed to the costs of "making money" on the deal.

I soon faced other mounting financial problems-all stemming from efforts to save the farm business. For one thing, the 1988 seed corn did not germinate because of a seed defect. That cut corn production. Then, poor labor practices led to dry haulage (a low moisture hay silage) catching fire in its silo. Our net worth increased in spite of these problems due in large part to Frank's hard work, but by 1989, he had decided to leave Copake, so it was a difficult time for me. The mortgage I had worked out proved to be inadequate. I had used the value of the (moved) houses as a basis for my loans, but Farm Credit became uncooperative, and a one-year loan from Hudson City Savings was due. It was nearly time to plant in 1990, and I needed the money. I was told I was "making no money" and, in the words of the loan officer that, "it depends on the law suit."

It seemed to me that the small town law enforcement had created a credit problem and the banking systems had exchanged information, if not actual agreement on how to handle my situation. I questioned then, and I question now, the fiduciary integrity of the banks in sharing and revealing my financial status. I hadn't yet supplied an operating statement to HCS to get the one-year, $100,000 loan, yet their loan officer seemed to know. The same lawyer represented both HCS and Farm Credit, a bank that took 70 percent of my loan as a condition of release from debt payments to them.

FORWARD AND BACK WITH FIRE IN MIND

My lawyer, Jason Shaw, told me it was going to be very expensive and that it was important to find out what people witnessed as soon as possible while they still had a clear recollection of the details. I saw his point right away, and we went out there to talk with the people who had seen the fire first. Fran Dick was first.

She said the only person she actually saw was Frank, who had left the scene an hour beforehand and no one else came in or went out of the barn. This proved to be damaging since she was the only on-site witness anytime near the time of the fire. She had been sitting on the front porch, which offered a full view of the north-south wing of the barn. The east-west wing sat behind the old horse barn. The driveway was in full view. She said she had seen a wisp of white smoke rise up over the front barn, and she got up and walked to the driveway at the side of the house for a better look at where the smoke was coming from. High up in the haymow there was a little door, and she saw the smoke coming out there. It was on the east end of the barn. She ran into the house to call in the fire. While she was on the phone, Fran Dick heard an explosion. When she came back outside, the entire east-west wing of the barn was in flames. Jason recorded what she said on paper and had her read it over. Then, he had her draw a diagram of the scene. Jason made sure she was satisfied with the statement and the drawing before he put his Notary Public stamp on the document.

Next, we got a statement from Larry Dick. He had been in the house just after supper, when his wife noticed the fire. While she was on the phone, he rushed out to witness flames blasting straight out of the center of the barn. He too drew a diagram of what he'd seen; it showed one door, while four doors actually existed, two each on east and west sides of the barn.

Bill Carol, a neighbor, was working in the yard when he heard Fran Dick yell about the barn being on fire. His observations matched hers closely, and he had gone inside to call in the fire as the explosion occurred, too. When he came out, the whole place was in flames.

The next day Tom Budd from Farm Credit called me. He had been working with me on financing farm operations, and his company held the mortgage on nearly everything I owned. It was good news when he said they'd lend me money to pay for the new barn. I owned 380 acres that they valued at $5,000 an acre, and the debt level was quite low, so I was pleased. Then, the bad news: no money for lawyer's fees. The cost of a trial was estimated to be as high as $50,000, and that added to my worries. With them tying up all my assets where was I supposed to get money to pay the lawyers? Then I got more bad news. Tom informed me that the loan would go above his limit, making it necessary for a new loan officer to manage the deal.

That news came just in time for the Fireman's Convention, complete with a village parade led by none other than Sheriff Paul Proper. I really became conscious of the small circle of community players tightening around me. I would have to face the very individuals I held in suspicion of trying to ruin me.

Parade day found me watching the greenhouse. The tent was up and the usual racy entertainment you would expect at an all male gathering was arranged. To make matters worse the festivities were going to take place on my farm right behind the firehouse. I went to a lot of trouble to harvest the hay just at the right time so they could use my field. I was invited to join the sheriff and others at the firehouse clubroom, but I just couldn't do it. The arrest, the rebuilding loan and the pressure to squeeze every dollar weighed heavily on me. Parades and beers weren't going to solve my problems in the community or steady my nerves.

The lot in front of the greenhouse was on Church Street and I put up a sign for $5 parking as was done the last time the parade was in town. The parade was about to start. The last time I had cleared $200 for the parking. Too bad I was competing against my own free parking on land behind the firehouse. I only took in $50. Attendance was off a little because of Frank being arrested for arson. I desperately needed cash for lawyers and I felt like an outcast from the village. It didn't matter that I knew Frank was innocent, and even if it were proven, would the community believe it. It was going to be a tough row to hoe.

The crowd gathered along the street, but it was quiet, even sullen. I walked the thin line of parade watchers as the large golf cart carrying the sheriff cruised up Church Street. The sheriff was dressed to the max in his uniform, shiny shoes and polished paraphernalia. I wanted to splatter the pompous bastard with a tomato. He wasn't ten feet away when he glanced toward me and then looked quickly away. It was an "I took care of you" look. I was facing a huge task and I felt bad all around. I even felt bad that the convention would probably bypass Copake in the years to come.

Days later, I climbed the open stairway from the foyer of Jason Shaw's law firm in Hudson to his office. I was very upset with the way Frank had been arrested, and I expressed myself straightforwardly, I'm sure. Shaw wasn't moved. He coldly said 95 percent of everyone arrested was guilty. In other words, arrest nearly equaled guilt. I protested that Frank had not had a lawyer present during the questioning, and Shaw replied that the police needed to be allowed leeway in order to do their jobs. I couldn't believe what I was hearing, and insisted on a hearing in Copake. If the only evidence they had against Frank was that bogus confession, then there wouldn't be a case, and it would be thrown out of court. So, we went forward.

In early August, we got our hearing. Shaw, Frank and I arrived at the town hall to a large crowd. Cars and pick-ups lined the street. After we'd found parking, I walked back to the front door and spotted the big van from the Office of Fire Prevention and Control, and guess who was leaning against the van, holding court with a group of townsfolk? There wasn't anything I could do about it. It was "dirty pool" because John Morgan in his uniform and the big van set the tone for the hearing. Everyone that walked past the van got the clear massage the State of New York, with all its prestige, said they finally got the arsonist. Remember, Morgan was not even going to testify. He was there only for show.

Inside, Justice of the Peace Kane presided over a standing room only courtroom. He announced that it was a preliminary hearing, and he proceeded to read the arson charges filed by Investigator Cozzolino. At that point, Jason Shaw requested that the press be excluded so that the case would not be tried in the papers. Shaw had reviewed the confession Frank had been forced to sign. The statement included details of the barn fire of 1985 that Frank was also accused of starting. In that case, he had supposedly left a light on in the feed room. The light, "close to paper and dust balls," was described as heating and igniting the papers and dust, causing the fire. It was so obviously an unlikely cause of any fire that the charges were made in that fire. But

Jason believed those statements alone, if published, could give the impression that Frank had started that fire, thus making a fair trial in the area virtually impossible.

The first witness was Scott Hedges, and he described the fire and how a falling beam had hurt him. The DA apparently highlighted the danger of the fire with this witness, then, on cross examination, Shaw established the origin of the fire at the north end of the barn. He also tried to establish that no real investigation of the fire had occurred, but the line of questioning seemed to go nowhere. A partial victory came with the request of the court for the reporter from the Independent to leave the courtroom, and then the DA called Investigator Cozzolino to the stand.

I was told not to say anything, but I was boiling mad when Cozzolino took the stand. Cozzolino threw several nervous glances in my direction as if he thought I was going to erupt. Cozzolino told the court that he had met Frank in the sheriff's office, and he made the point that Frank was told he could leave at any time. The door "was open." I fumed at that statement. Frank was 20 miles away and they sent his ride away. Besides, Frank told Sheriff Proper he would not go to the sheriff's office unless I went with him. They had lied to get him there by himself so they could grill him. Cozzolino recalled how he had asked Frank about his activities on the day of the fire. Frank, he said, told him how he had taken a cigarette, lit it, and flicked it into the hay mound. I felt my blood pressure rise again; a city person might call it a "hay mound," but a farmer knows only a haymow. I bristled when he said that. The DA asked Cozzolino to further describe exactly how Frank had walked around his truck to get the cigarette out of the glove box, lit it and flicked it into the mow. She also asked him if Frank had seen the statement, read it, understood it. Had Frank been read his rights? During the affirmative answers, I kept thinking of the absurdity of the whole confession and how the language in it revealed its true author. I was glaring at him, right then; Cozzolino smoked but Frank did not.

Shaw got in some cross-examination, asking if Cozzolino had known or been told anything about Frank that would make him prone to suggestion. He also asked Cozzolino if he had been involved in any other aspects of an investigation, but specifically, Shaw was after Cozzolino's role in drafting the confession statement, and Cozzolino said he "didn't recall whether suggestions of his influenced the statement as written." Shaw even asked if profanity was used on Frank to get him to sign the statement. The DA, of course, got in objections throughout the questioning, and as Judge Kane denied Shaw's motion to dismiss the charges, ordering instead that Frank be held for the grand jury, I felt like we had lost ground.

A shroud of guilt covered Frank. The paper covered the damages of the fire as told by Scott Hedges and reported that Frank would be held for a grand jury. For me, it was agony. Shaw wasn't able to establish that the confession was involuntary. Cozzolino slipped by. The hearing only provided more fodder for the rumor mill. The only evidence, the statement of confession, didn't add up. The term "hay mound" was not one Frank would use and he didn't smoke. Why would anyone who didn't smoke use a cigarette to start a fire, and why would Frank say there was hay in the mow when he knew it was corn stover bedding and not hay? Besides, why would he want to burn the barn anyway, his whole future depended on the barn and the cows. Many of the cows were his! There was also no real investigation done, but somehow that didn't seem to matter. I began to see where it was headed. The District Attorney had someone, and guilt and innocence, facts and circumstances, could all be manipulated in court for the desired outcomes.

The next day, I stood in front of the free stall barn with Bill Bradway wondering what to do about building the milk house and flat barn. Then the part-time carpenter who worked at the store as a butcher drove up and leaned out of his car window. He said he'd heard I couldn't get anyone to build my cow barn, so he offered to do it for $10,000 more than I estimated the total cost. He demanded to be paid before starting the job, plus he demanded that I had to supply the lumber. He said, "You know how to get in touch with me-take it or leave it." Then he drove off. Bill Bradway was as mad as I was. Bill and I talked it over, but he had us over a barrel. Bill said he couldn't build the milk house but he could do the rest. He suggested we get that built first, and then I'd fire him. It seemed complicated and expensive, but we got him to agree to do it in stages then I wrote the check and ordered the lumber so we could get on with it.

At the same time, my lawyer called to talk about the subdivision of my land. The buyer, still wanted the land, but he dropped his offer well below the price we agreed on before. Griffin pointed out the value of the subdivision was solid and advised me to turn down the offer. I took his advice, reluctantly. I thought a counter offer might have worked to bring a little better price, but no counter offer was pursued

For the next couple of weeks Frank's case languished and he became scared that he would be jailed. He wanted a new lawyer, so I called Griffin and discussed Frank's concerns. He came to the house the next day and brought Jason Shaw along to talk about the case and Shaw's qualifications. He had worked in New York City as an Assistant DA and handled arson cases, and he said he'd do whatever we wanted as far as our case was concerned. Maybe the clincher was his willingness to work with the payments. If I changed lawyers, it would definitely require coming up with more cash. And, I knew the bank wouldn't lend me any money for legal expenses. I felt trapped. Frank was not happy, but I decided to stick with the firm of Rapport, Myers, Griffin and Whitbeck. Shaw promised more action. "I will do anything you want done," he said.

COMPETING CONCLUSIONS

I had to counteract the police claim the fire was started by a cigarette tossed into the haymow by my son. It was established that the fire started on the east end of the old barn. The police claimed he flicked a cigarette through an open door some 12 feet above the ground. That seemed unlikely. They claimed that he checked the dry cows across the road, went back to his truck to get a cigarette, lit it, and flicked the cigarette as he drove out. He didn't smoke so that too seemed unlikely. Since the truck was parked by the milk house at the rear of the barn, the door would have been on the wrong side. He would have had to stop the truck, get out and walk to the other side of the truck to even have a chance to flick a lit cigarette through the door. The police countered the fact that the fire didn't start until an hour after he left by saying the fire smoldered unnoticed for an hour. Then there was the problem of the corncrib being on fire when the firemen arrived. It was at the north-west corner, far away from the south-east corner where the fire started. I couldn't see any way a cigarette flicked through a door on the south end could start the corncrib fire on the west end that stood on the other side of the driveway.

All of this was confirmed much later when my fire investigator examined photos taken by Bull Call. They clearly show an absence of fire intense enough to ignite the corncrib standing some 35 feet north of the barn. He said the fire was consistent with an accelerant being used to start the fire. The fire flared up very intensely setting the corncrib on fire. Then the accelerant burned out and the fire died back. That was when the picture was taken. He thought a small fire was set on the east end and something like gas was spread on the west end. Then he asked me to examine how a candle burns. It is not the melted wax that burns. It isn't even the wick that burns. He explained. If you look closely the flame is above the wick. It is the gases that evaporate from the wick that burns and supports the flame, he said. He likened the situation of how the fire started on a gas stove with a pilot light. When the vapor from the gas reached the flame from the corn stover everything ignited in a violet blast. He estimated that it would only take a gallon of gas—two at most—to started the fire.

He said anyone in the building at that time would have been killed. While there was one other possible escape route, I concluded the open door was the most likely, and that he had to be on the ground when the explosion took place. It was then that he was hit by the fire blasting out the door in the direction of the corncrib.

The 1985 fire racked up a $425,000 loss. In addition to the barn itself, that included lost stock, equipment and all the machines and tools needed to keep a farm business going. It didn't cover lost milk production that would hang on for almost a year. The Bull Spring fire two years later revealed similarities between the two fires. Most strikingly, it was officially determined that it was accidental, caused by an electrical malfunction in the calf room. In fact, photos taken of the scene by my younger son showed the calf room had no flames while the rest of the barn was in almost total flames. In each case, the intensity and suddenness of the flames indicated to me the use of an accelerant. The first fire was witnessed to be back by the silos, but the most violent fire was on the other end of the barn. After the fires were put out there was another similarity. Part of the haymow floors was still there where the fire was first seen in each fire, but everything was gone at the other end of the barn. It was, as Henry Call said, as if the fire moved.

We had to prove that the official version of how the fire started was wrong. I had to start somewhere.

THE SEARCH FOR TRUTH

I sat at the kitchen table, the statement of confession spread out before me. I'd had a week more to think about it and the whole business made less sense than ever. The statement said a cigarette tossed into hay started the fire. I did not doubt it would a bit; still I felt every detail had to be tested. Would a cigarette really start a fire if it were dropped into hay? Would it happen an hour later?

I went over to the barn, got some hay and walked down to the Circle Deli to buy a pack of cigarettes. When I returned home with my little kit of fire starters, I opened the wood stove and inserted the hay, following up with a lit cigarette. I fully expected it to start a fire in just a few minutes. I started my stopwatch. Ten minutes later, it went out. No hay burned. I repeated the process, but this time, I pushed the cigarette down into the hay instead of letting it lie on top. It went out. Then I opened the draft on the stove to make a steady flow of air across the burning cigarette. No fire. I used the entire pack of 20 cigarettes and not one fire resulted. In fact, each one burned out in about ten minutes. I called Jason Shaw with the results of my experiment.

The next day, he called back in a very upbeat mood. He had talked with a former state police investigator who had taught arson detection for firemen. Ralph Fuentes was the man, and he was reputed to be the best arson investigator in the state. He worked with a partner out of Syracuse for Loss Analysis, Inc., and in addition to the work he had done for the state, he also worked for insurance companies. Shaw had consulted with him about our case and what Fuentes had told Shaw gave me a boost. "I can tell you how it didn't start," he'd said, "it didn't start by a cigarette thrown in hay."

His explanation made perfect sense. Hay stems crisscross in a way that supports the cigarette above the surface of the hay by two or three stems. That means air between the cigarette and combustible material insulates the material from the cigarette enough to prevent kindling temperature, and thus the fire cannot ignite. Even if a stem burns down from right under the cigarette, it goes so fast that there's not enough heat to generate a fire. He said it is different than when a person falls asleep with a cigarette in his hand. In that case the cigarette is pushed down into the fabric so as to generate more heat. Fuentes agreed to help with the case, but he wanted a bank check for $500. I was happy with the breakthrough and headed out the door and down the sidewalk toward the new Hudson City Savings Bank office that had just opened next to Brad Peck's insurance office.

Ralph Fuentes and Jason Shaw pulled into my farm driveway in a shiny van and got out to meet me. Fuentes, tall and muscular, commanded respect, and stopped long enough to take a small blood pressure pill. We had friendly talk as we crossed the street to my place and the kitchen table where we would discuss the statement of confession and the case. Fuentes reviewed the statement and listened to my rendition of the surrounding events. It was clear to him that Frank should have been read his rights when he got into the car. Frank should have been told that he would be questioned about the fire. It was clear that Morgan had been contacted the day before to come down and interrogate Frank about the fire. Earlier, Frank had agreed to go to the sheriff's office only if I went along. They intended to get Frank alone, and to get a statement out of him that they knew could not be admitted in a trial. Although Fuentes was certainly sympathetic, he knew it would be tough to reverse the kind of damage done. Support for the police is almost universal. My own father had just about summed it up when he said after the arrest, "They shut you up, didn't they?"

I had a small office in the back of my house. The paneled wall held a big four-foot square map of the farm and the town. I could look out across my back fields through the big window, and it was here that I sat at A.D.'s desk, planning the spring planting. I also worried and worked over the problems surrounding Frank's arrest. How Paul Proper could do such a thing, kept at me. I was sitting at the desk one day wondering about that when a scene of the sheriff pulling into a neighbor's yard came from the back of my memory. I could hear someone ask if he ever arrested someone he knew was innocent. I could picture his gray Chrysler clearly, but I couldn't piece the whole conversation together. I wrote what I remembered on a slip of paper and stuck it into one of the desk's cubbyholes. It was something I came back to from time to time. I would take out the paper, read it and if I remembered more of the conversation I would write it down.

I became convinced that my memory would restore the incident if I concentrated on it long enough.

The real problem was that I hadn't given it my full attention at the time it actually happened. After I began applying my concentration, things took shape. Looking at the note I had pigeon-holed helped. After several months of reviewing my notes I felt I could reconstruct the entire incident. One thing bothered me. In my mind's eye I could see Proper roll a cigar in his finger tips even though I couldn't remember seeing him smoke. But the essential scene took place while I was trimming my bushes on a summer evening and a gathering of neighbors chatted on the Stang porch nearby. Proper arrived in his hardtop Chrysler with the windows down and parked the car. My neighbors gathered around the car in friendly fashion and I joined them. We tossed local issues and rumors back and forth for a while until the subject of the sheriff's job came up. Somebody asked the sheriff if he ever arrested a person he knew was innocent. Proper mused some and said, "No, but it is done sometimes. You do it in the interest of public safety. You have to maintain control of the situation. If you lose control bad things can happen." What happens when it comes up for trial, he was asked. "That's not so easy," he said, "But if it comes up you just screw it all up." That's how I remember it, exactly.

That reply brought the group of us to an impasse. We didn't get it. Proper continued to explain that when the DA figures out what happened he just drops everything and doesn't go any further. What happens if sheriff has to take the stand? What then? That isn't so easy, the sheriff answered, but if they do get you on the stand you just say you did it." When you are under oath you always tell the truth.

The person asking shook his head in disbelief and said he couldn't do that. All Paul Proper did was shrug. Then he said, "You just say you did it in the interest of public safety." He emphasized that you can't lose control of the situation, if you do, bad things can happen. Then he said, Once a case gets to court everything straightens out. He made a motion with his hand. The system works, he said. Then someone asked about damages. Proper explained that damages are high because the case is never cleared up. The DA just drops it so no conclusion is reached. The person arrested is never cleared of the crime. That's what makes the damages so high: half a million, maybe a million. Then there was a pause. I could see him roll his cigar as he thought. Then he added, maybe even a million and a half in a real bad one. Then the question of who pays was asked. His answer was, "The insurance company pays."

Sheriff Proper made it clear that each sheriff in the state gets one, but only one. He said, "Any more and they won't pay." Then Sheriff Paul Proper told us, that he hadn't used his yet, but he was going to "give it to someone before I leave office." He added, "You have to be careful about who you do it to, because if it goes wrong, it comes out bad, real bad." Then the conversation drifted to other things.

As I began to reconstruct the conversation I could see how Frank's arrest could have been tailored to fit the sheriff's definition of protecting public safety. It certainly put him back in control. I could see how his arrest took the heat off the sheriff's office. It made a certain kind of logical sense, and coupled with my anger and the damages done, it made me determined to sue for damage. Even if there was a trial and a finding of not guilty, Frank would be followed by suspicion all his life.

VIDEO GAMES

To further demonstrate that the fire could not have been started by a cigarette tossed into the haymow, Jason Shaw suggested that we make a video with Ralph Fuentes to show how far-fetched the theory actually was. Personally, I favored gathering a little hay right there in the courtroom, but Jason vetoed that idea because of the risk. I suppose if it did catch fire, we'd have a smoke and fire call emergency. Even though I believed the odds were heavily in our favor, I agreed to try the video strategy.

Jason planned to locate a video service and apply for a certified weather report from the weather bureau to establish the temperature at the time of the fire. I had to assemble the various materials, including chopped corn stover, the only fuel present in the haymow where the fire started. The only trouble was that it was now October and not June when farms typically had corn stover. I did find some at a neighboring farm though.

When the day to shoot the video came, we had trouble matching temperatures with the actual reported temperature from the day of the fire. We set up production inside the milking flat barn still under construction. We stood around as the heaters brought up the temperature. Finally, Fuentes decided it was okay to proceed, and we spent the rest of the day running fire starting drills with both hay and corn stover. By the end of the afternoon, we were convinced that we could completely discredit the statement about how the fire started with the flick of a cigarette. At $350 an hour, I sure hoped we had the job done right.

Soon afterwards, we met in Jason Shaw's office, and I told him I wanted to sue for damages. He seemed to explode with disapproval. "Nice people don't sue," he said. I was momentarily stunned. Then, I reiterated how the arrest had taken place and that it was illegal and that no evidence other than the phony statement were presented. He argued that I couldn't sue for the way the statement had been forced "because the police have to have some leeway or they can't do their job." Obviously, he refused to take up a suit, and that meeting ended. I was not pleased with the outcome.

At a later meeting in Hudson, I met Ralph Fuentes at Jason's office. The State had apparently saved the electrical box from the

Bull Spring fire as evidence. Ralph wanted to examine it to get a better idea of how the fire started. Nancy Snyder, the Assistant DA, arranged for John Morgan to be there. I met him up close for the first time. I was surprised that he was shorter than I expected. In contrast to Ralph who was dressed to dig around at a fire site, John was dressed for a court appearance, shiny, tasseled shoes and all.

On the way over, Ralph explained that by tracking the sequence of fuse burnouts, it was possible to determine the progression of the fire. If one of the circuits started the fire, it would look different than if the fire had burned through the insulation and caused the burnout. Morgan acted pretty smug as Fuentes knelt down to examine the fuse box with a flashlight. Morgan's smugness irritated Fuentes, and the dislike of the two for each other was apparent to me. In the process, Ralph found three blown circuits and he asked Morgan where they went. Morgan explained that Bull Call, who worked part-time for the police, had removed the box and hadn't marked the circuit connections. A trained investigator should have done that. All he could tell was that three circuits blew after the fire started. On the way back to the office, Ralph said that as the holder of the lease on the barn, only my approval should have released the box from the site. It became obvious to me that Sheriff Proper acted improperly when he ordered the fuse box removed on the night of the fire. Added to that, since I held the lease, Char Peck had the barn wreckage bulldozed, prematurely, if not illegally. So, it wasn't possible to determine where the blown circuits were connected, and for the most part, the whole exercise turned out to be a waste of time. A proper investigation couldn't be done.

I already knew Frank was innocent, but the stigma created by the arrest wouldn't go away just because we could discredit the confession. To a very large extent Frank had already been tried in the eye of the public. First there was the sheriff's news conference, and then the State Fire Control van parked at the courthouse door, then the police escorting Frank in front of the news cameras. Next, we faced the alleged motive-that of mental impairment. The apparent motive that appeared in some of the press was that Frank was a pyromaniac. Again, Jason called me into his office to discuss the matter. He proposed that we get a test done and have the results reported orally so that the State would not have access to a report. The fact no written report was made was a problem later on, but that will become apparent later in the story. We proceeded on his advice, and I waited in an Albany psychologist's office while Frank labored over a battery of tests. The doctor told me afterwards that Frank was not a pyromaniac, and that nothing he could find indicated that Frank had started any fires.

Still, Jason was not satisfied. He said he wanted a psychiatrist, a Ph.D., to do the test because it would carry more weight. We did it again as the bills piled up. In Saratoga Springs, I waited while Frank worked his way through the same tests, and the results indicated that Frank was not a pyromaniac. Jason talked with the doctor, too, but notes of the conversation did not appear later in the case files. But, we had our answers. The State had no motive, and no evidence, other than a half accurate statement by the fire truck driver, that Frank had any involvement with the Bull Spring Farm fire. Unfortunately for Frank, members of the fire company and most of the townspeople shunned him. One supporter was Dr. Layer, who didn't believe Frank started the fire because he loved his cattle too much. Other than that, friends, old and new, took their cues from the indictment. Anything I said was viewed with suspicion. Shortly, Jason received a plea bargain offer from the Assistant DA She would allow a six-month jail term and a payment to the Pecks for $25,000 to cover costs unmet by insurance. Jason rejected the offer immediately.

That didn't stop the calls demanding that I move my cows out of the Jenkins barn. It was tough, but things were coming together on this front. The flat barn was completed and the cows took to the new place as if they'd been there all their lives. We had half the milking machines, a third of the cost, and one person could still milk close to 40 cows an hour. That nearly matched the best we could do with the old milking parlor. The cows were out of the mud, we didn't have to pay rent, and we put in less time hauling feed. The farm work was done for the year, and a few finishing touches remained to be done on the outside of the milk house. It didn't solve my problems with sleeplessness however, and before long, the next bombshell hit.

Jason called with the news that our video evidence had been countered by a video made in John Morgan's garage. I headed in to Jason's office to see what he had. The video in question was made in Morgan's heated garage and as the hay smoldered the garage door was thrown open to create a draft. The hay burst into flames. Although Morgan's home video had no clock showing lapsed time and no record of the number of tests conducted was in evidence, there was enough to introduce a question of doubt that a cigarette couldn't have started the fire. The simple fact that a state investigator had carried out the experiment lent credibility, and even though Jason thought we could overcome the comparison, the damage was done. Jason put Morgan's video back in the file. That video caused a problem later on. Why Ralph Fuentes had told John Morgan about our video, neither Jason nor I knew, and, we were not pleased.

INTO THE AIR JUNIOR BIRDMAN

Airplanes fascinated many Copakians of the 1920s and '30s. Our big field provided a rough but adequate "airport" where flying and everything associated with it became cause for entertainment and excitement, and that included parachute jumping.

Jake Head decided he was going to try jumping, and he convinced Harvey Roberts to take him into the air. Jake, was young of course and had no training or experience. Jake got hold of a parachute and they announced the jump for a Sunday morning. A crowd gathered around our field to watch. The boys took off, circling the field, climbing to gain altitude. They dropped a test chute fashioned from a sheet to gauge the wind, and on the next pass, Jake jumped. He fully expected to land in front of the crowd.

The wind had other ideas and Jake drifted over the town toward the Bristol house. Gladys Bristol was getting ready for church when heard a clattering on the roof. She looked out the window. Jake had landed on the roof and the chute snagged on the chimney. Jake was dangling in front of her bedroom window as he kicked and clawed trying to get hold of anything. She let out a big scream at the bizarre sight. She was still visibly shaken when the crowd showed up to rescue the Jake. It was most likely the first time Gladys had been late for church in her life.

A BURNING MAN AND THE FIRE REVISITED

It's a funny thing how your mind thinks backwards some-times. I drove my car right out to the Bull Spring fire from my place in town. I passed all the witnesses along Snyder Pond Road, and I even saw a guy out in my pasture. All I did was keep going to the barn to get my calves out. Later, as the facts became known, the scenes reassembled themselves. I could see it as plain as if it was movie. The witnesses got out of their cars not just to watch the fire, but also to watch the man run backward while he was watching the fire. He, the man with his arms raised, was the arsonist retreating from the fire. They either didn't get it or they didn't want to get involved. That the man running backward had set the same fire that captivated them. As far as I know, none of them reported it.

My memory took in the night of the fire. I retraced my steps. Frank was cooking a hamburger on the stove. The fire radio blared in his room, and Frank took off. I turned off the stove, but I was also talking on the phone when the siren blew. I heard the fire radio report that the fire was at Bull Spring Farm. That got to me. I got my shoes on and headed for the car, squealing the tires on the way down the driveway. I could see smoke as I rounded the curve onto Center Hill Road, past the firehouse. I slowed down for the bridge at Brown's Pond, and as I headed up the hill I looked out my car window and spotted a man standing in my pasture. Then I looked back at the road. Something seemed odd so I turned toward the pasture again; I remember wondering what the guy was doing there. Parked cars lined the road and a group of people stood along the fence to my pasture and hay field. They were watching the fire. The man in the pas-ture, his hands raised, seemed to have walked out there to get a better look. Then with the car back at top speed I looked ahead at the fire. I was sure it was arson this time. I was mad and I was going to demand an investigation.

I saw fire trucks already in position at the entrance to the barn, so I parked out of their way just past the Skip Lilly place where his family was eating. I headed across the field to get the calves out, but I was simmering mad about the ongoing lack of action in catching the arsonist. Much later I slowly pieced the events together in my mind, I realized that the man in the field had not simply walked out there to get a better view; He was walking backward, looking at the fire he'd started. And, the people rubbernecking were watching the arsonist. Two questions haunted me. When I thought about it, I concluded that they watched the arsonist coming from the fire. Why didn't they come forward? The second question was how did he get past the Lilly family without being noticed?

In the meantime, a note taken by investigator Walter Shook indicated Arthur Coleman, Jr. did report what he saw. It gave credence to the arsonist fleeing the fire. Coleman reported that he had driven past a man headed away from the site in a blue Toyota pick-up. Coleman said he could smell burning flesh from the other man's vehicle as he passed close by. I asked Shaw to follow-up on the report and he finally got enough information from the prosecutor's office to substantiate the story. As Coleman slowed down to navigate the sharp corner on Snyder Pond Road, he came very close to the truck coming from the opposite direction. The driver of the truck was so badly burned Coleman reported, that he could smell his burning flesh. Shook's conclusion was that the man got burned when he started the fire. It was the only way he could have been at that location at that time. Although Shook checked all nearby hospitals, he turned up no leads on the guy. Still, he determined the report was factual. I knew Frank was innocent anyway, but the story of the burning man showed Investigator Walter Shook knew too. The question of how someone torched the barn and escaped unseen by the Lilly family would not go away. Even with all the circumstantial scenarios and supporting evidence, I would still have to convince myself before I could be 100 percent sure of convincing others. I've learned one thing in this life-other people aren't as concerned with your problems as you are. They can be lead to the water but they won't drink unless they want to.

REENACTING THE FIRE: THE LAST QUESTION ANSWERED

I waited until the April snow melted. It was a good day to test my theory that no one could have escaped the notice of the Lilly family after setting the fire. It was warm and sunny. The grass was green already and it hadn't rained for a few days. I drove up to Snyder Pond Road and parked where Bull Spring Brook runs under the road. I made my way up along the brook to the landfill and decided which way to go from there. It seemed logical to head east of the swamp and woods, so I walked as close to the woods as possible, but the Lilly's picnic table was in full view. My feet got wet from the layer of water laying on the hard-pan below the surface. I couldn't see how the arsonist could have gone this way without being observed. I expected the swamp had been even wetter.

After I got to where the barn had been and I placed myself right where the arsonist had to be standing ten months earlier. The only difference between then and now was that the haymow would have been four and half feet high and the open door would have been in front of me. To my right I saw Center Hill Road and the driveway to the farmhouse. Fuentes had said the arsonist would have been killed if he'd been inside the barn, so I knew the guy was close to the barn, on the ground when the fire blasting through the doorway burned him. But at that moment, Fran Dick was on the phone and wouldn't have seen him. Bill Carroll was on the phone, too. Possibly, Larry Dick might have spotted him from the other side of the fire blast, but it was unlikely. Of course, I remembered where I was when the siren blew, and it would have been right about the same time the man was burned form the blasting fire.

Using the stopwatch function on my wristwatch, I started my reenactment. It took 4 seconds to slip down the creek bank and get out of sight behind the barn. In 12 seconds, I was in sight of the road, moving through what would have been a spread out herd of cows in the pasture. I kept going along a logical route from there and in 40 seconds I found myself standing next to Bull Spring Brook. But I was standing on a mound of dirt piled up from the dredging of the creek years before. I hadn't noticed it before. I looked toward the Lilly picnic table, but it was blocked from view by the woods. A dry path leads to the heart of Bull Spring Swamp, and I followed it to an easy jump over a narrow stream. I landed on the backside of the landfill and out of sight. I kept moving down until I got to the pasture and the spot north of the bush along the fence where I saw the man. I checked my watch again. Because I knew the time the siren blew, I could determine where the man was standing at about 8:15. Guess what? I stood on the same ground, same spot, same time.

I returned to the house to retrace my steps. By timing my movements from the first sound of the siren, when I searched for my shoes, to getting into the car, driving to the fire and spotting the man in the field, I confirmed the time I saw him. 8:15! Arthur Coleman reported seeing the guy in the truck at about 8:30. I had been wrong about a person not being able to escape unseen. I knew how he'd gotten in and out.

He went in the north wing of the barn and up haymow ladder. The corn stover was right there and he started a pilot fire there, on the east end of the barn. Then, he climbed over a beam into the haymow on the west end to spread the gasoline he'd brought along. He planned to jump the four and a half feet out the door to the ground, but Fran Dick could be seen standing in his driveway, so he held back. Then, Bill Carroll appeared. The coast cleared, but not before the man had been burned by the ignition of the gas fumes. He probably hit the ground seconds ahead of the blast and had to take the same route I had sleuthed, but his neck and arms were burned, making him identifiable on his drive past Coleman. And, ironically, the burns made that indelible image in my memory of the backward-running man, his arms raised in pain.

As I said the similarities to my 1985 fire and Bull Spring fire were uncanny. The fire was first sighted on one end of the barn, but the most intense burning occurred where the gas was spread on the other end. Fire was first spotted by the silos in the 1985 fire, but the most intense burning happened by the milking parlor. Dell Walton, fire chief at the time, requested an investigation. Had one actually been done, it would have confirmed a crime, and that gas or similar combustible had been used to burn that barn. Intervention by someone, with the power of Sheriff Proper, was the only way the investigation could have been thwarted without the fire chief knowing about it. One of the insurance adjusters told me an assessment is made on each fire insurance policy to fund the state Office of Fire Prevention and Control and they are on call 24 hours a day.

I had demanded an investigation the night of the fire at Bull Spring. Sheriff Proper arranged for Frank and me to go to his office to take lie detector tests. That same night, I had told Investigator Shook that I suspected George Partridge's hired man was the arsonist, and Shook's reaction indicated to me that Shook had investigated him for an incident before. Was he the fireman who had recently been given the lie detector test? Shook wrote in his notes later that night that "Langdon had no suspect." Did he know this man could not have done it? Why did he write I had no suspect? What did Investigator Walter Shook know that he was not telling?

Everything indicated to me that the investigation was stopped mid-week. Shook investigated what Coleman saw and determined that the driver of the blue Toyota started the fire. He determined that it was not Frank. Further, Char Peck called the sheriff's office to ask if they were done with their investigation. Proper approved the bulldozing of the fire site, giving more credence to the fact that he did not want a full investigation done to prove a crime was committed. Apparently he didn't want to arrest the man that burned my barn. The fact that Shook checked hospitals for burn victims but apparently failed to check state motor vehicle records for the Toyota, also indicated that he, or possibly Sheriff Proper, knew who owned such a truck. Additionally, the fact that Proper did not do the lie detector test means he no longer considered Frank a likely suspect. His arrest of Frank was to shut me up. My campaign on behalf of the community to gather information leading to the apprehension of the arsonist must have rubbed someone the wrong way, put pressure on a sensitive point. The real arsonist was being protected, and since Proper had nothing to lose, the insurance company lined up to pay for any damages and for his defense, he could claim his actions were in the interest of public safety. He knew I had suffered great losses from arson, but I don't think he cared if I collected damages or not.

The damage no court could reverse was the social kind. The town's people pulled back, and Franks arrest was considered a "personal problem." To be separated and shunned from our heritage and livelihood in Copake, marked our family in ways that were unpredictable and long lasting. Anger and regret grew from the false arrest and what I still claim to be a malicious arrest. The problems that evolved took on the nature of anything but a personal problem. It was a systemic problem. It was one that a poor citizen like me would be hard-pressed to solve.

I believed in the courts and the lawyers. I believed that the system worked, but I found they were part of the problem, not the solutions. Can I prove a cover-up of the Copake arsons if the lawyers and courts are part of a cover-up?

LOVE'S POSSIBLE COUNTRY

After the trauma of my third fire, Bull Spring, the arrest of my son and the subsequent dropping of charges, I was simply burned out. My children pooled enough money together to send me to Florida where I could be with Mom and Dad for Christmas. It was a good way to end 1988, as the pressure seemed to melt away in the warm sunshine on the beach. And, I discovered a couple of important things. First, I had developed high blood pressure, and second, there was more to life than what I had just experienced in Copake. After a week, a seriously long break for a farmer, I felt thoroughly refreshed. Right after I returned home, things indeed got brighter for me.

Donna Peck stopped by for a visit and told me about a good friend of hers who was having a hard time of it nearby. The friend's name was Cassandra and she was a baker who worked at the Ancramdale Store. She learned a lot about baking at Sara Bests Foods in New York. She also did the baking for the famous Red Lion Inn in Stockbridge, Massachusetts. The Inn was located right down the street from the Norman Rockwell house, and I couldn't resist the temptation to stop by to try the baked goods and to meet Cassandra.

She was full of energy. I loved her smile and she was easy to talk with. I asked her to go to a dance with me, and things went well from the beginning. Her life seemed as complex as mine, but we shared a love of the country and when I showed her the greenhouse, she took to it right away. She began stopping by after work, and her imaginative flair transformed it into an interesting place. Together we developed a corner of the greenhouse where a fountain and plants made a lively display. "Cassie" located some old counters from a Hudson hat shop. We went to a fabric outlet and purchased some bright materials. Together we fashioned a sales counter complete with an awning. People liked the effect and Cassie had fun visiting with them.

At the same time, the nearby savings bank was expanding and two adjacent houses were purchased so the houses could be removed and the bank could move ahead on its plans for a new building. Contracts for the removal of the houses were put out, and I was in a good position to bid on them. It was estimated that

I would double my money, and Farm Credit was pleased about that even though they would only finance the project for one year. I had a problem understanding what their problem was. I certainly needed the money, and the houses bordered my farm. I won the contract dated May 11, and the moving operation began the first of June.

Cassie and I were investing too, in our relationship. We decided to put our fortunes, the bright and the tarnished, together in a quiet marriage ceremony the end of May. So, the housing deal fit right in with our domestic partnership. One night we were with the Justice of the Peace, and the next day the Larmon House Movers and their big equipment jump-started us on the road to the future. We planned to position one house on Empire Road near the pond behind the village. The pond was originally dug for fire protection years before but it had filled in to where it was of little value. We had the contractor dig it out to raise the house site. That would make a three-acre home site from where a deck would overlook the pond.

It seemed simple enough. Frank would run the farm while I dealt with the moving project. Cassie would go to her job as usual and we'd all make out fine. A harbinger of things to come hit us the first day. Cassie returned from her job in Ancramdale around noon. Her boss had demanded that she stop "the arsonist" from coming to the store because it was bad for business. Cassie quit on the spot. Then, we needed to compensate for the loss of income, and we thought she could work in the greenhouse and do some baking on the side. We bought a commercial oven, and together we planned a rustic post and beam building for the front of the greenhouse. It would keep the farm theme and be a good place for her to build up the baking business. With her foundation of over a thousand valuable cookbooks, Cassie wanted to hold cooking classes. Despite the challenges of the summer I felt happier than ever.

The moving job looked like it would be profitable, but there would be trade-offs. Frank's sole direction of the farm operations pitted him against employees who refused many times to take any direction because they held the suspicion of arson against him. The house-moving project hit a few snags, expensive snags. The Pectal house, planned for relocation to Empire Road got hung up on its framing while a complaint and stop work order initiated by the next door neighbors was resolved. The dredging of the pond that I thought would provide extra fill for the site, in addition to a nice view from the deck of the house, disagreed with the Millers' (neighbors) nose for any pollution that might threaten their well. The irony of the situation was that I had to show the building inspector the Millers leach field. It was filled with raw sewage, and it was leaking onto my property. They were able to hire a backhoe to install ten feet of pipe. I wasn't so lucky. Because my project qualified as new construction, I had to hire an engineer. The stop work order cost me between $15,000 and $20,000. I realized a change of location might facilitate the move even as it cut its potential monetary value of being next to the pond. We moved the house to the corner of the road with the hill rising behind it.

The footing was dug for the foundation and just as the pouring was about to begin, the building inspector reappeared with a complaint that we were too close to the road. Out came the tape measures and the time-honored pacing of distances. Because of the curve in the road one corner was a foot to close. To avoid further quibbling, I recalled Larmon and his equipment so we could move the house another two feet and satisfy the complaint.

Although it was never finished because of the stop work order, we graded the yard and moved the barn closer to the pond. Cassie eventually wanted to remodel it into a usable place with a kitchen where she could teach her cooking classes. We managed to uncover a large rectangular limestone slab that made a wonderful bench and we planted a perennial garden around it. Cassie liked sitting down there and I kept the grass mowed. With a few newly planted fruit trees and the old outhouse providing storage for my fishing pole and a quaint atmosphere, it was a great place to unwind after work. Keep in mind, the greenhouse was a full 7 day a week job from mid-February until late fall.

The house-moving project served to offer some real hope after the fire losses and the arrest. Farm Credit would only fund it for one year, but Hudson City Savings reluctantly picked it up for an additional year. They said it all hinged on the lawsuit. The never-ending problems involved not just the finances of the farming operation but, I believe, the lawsuit. Stop work orders complicated the house moving operation and took up most of my time, but that didn't stop us from dreaming. Frank envisioned the big view location for the blue house. To get it up to where it would overlook the valley, a road had to be built into the side of the hill. Once situated, the bow window in the living room would look north; double French doors would replace the kitchen fireplace and open to the view over the Taconic Mountains. Of course the driveway was a problem, but what a view!

Donna Peck brought a tenant who would carry the cost with the rent, and we thought we had it made. Then, the tenant heard rumors about Frank being the "Copake Arsonist." He called to demand I keep Frank away from the place. That was actually impossible to do with our cows in the pasture right next to the house. The tenant went to my lawyer and raised hell about the lease before he moved out owing us several months in back rent. We were lucky enough to get a second tenant but unlucky enough to have him refuse to allow prospective buyers into the house when we had a chance to sell it.

In the meantime, the dairy industry was not doing well in the Northeast. Farm Credit was quick to inform me, and in response they suspended the making of new loans for dairies. When I submitted my annual operating statement I detected a chilly mood. It had not been a great year. The house move had not helped the farm, and a silo fire had destroyed a great deal of haylage the year before. This year, the crop inventory was much better giving a rise in net worth for the farm, but the cash flow was negative. I made a point of the growth in net worth, not just due to the house move, but because of the larger crop inventory. I was countered with the one-time nature of the house move. The farm, according to the bank, was not going to warrant any additional loan money.

A new possibility appeared in the form of a neighbor who wanted to purchase an acre from a previously subdivided parcel, and I figured it might be a way to raise $10,000. After another visit with the bank I was not convinced they would not help much. The bank wanted 10 grand to release the land from the mortgage, and they informed me that I would have to get $30,000 for the acre. At that rate, the entire block was worth over three million. What I needed was cash for operations and equipment replacement. I was not getting help from Farm Credit. Other local banks were not making farm loans. I felt that Frank's arrest was the big factor in the bank's decision, and I was left with few options. Odyssey Farm agreed to a deal to plant corn in exchange for the use of a parcel of my excess land. It was the only way I could keep the farm going.

After the greenhouse business slowed down, Cassie and I decided to head for Maine for a few days. I had trouble putting the farm and money problems to rest, and the major problems with lawyers that caused huge damages nagged at me. Just as the Florida trip had helped ease the tension, the jaunt to Maine had a soothing effect on me. Cassie had always liked Maine, and it made our stay in Kennebunkport all the more special. It's too bad we had to return to Copake so soon.

When we returned I sat for a while at A.D.'s big desk to mull things over in my head, a dangerous practice as it turned out. Then I called the New York State Bar Association in Albany. I told the receptionist that I needed a lawyer to sue another lawyer, on contingency, of course. I must have hit the magic nerve ending. She unleashed an accusatory barrage at me, never asking what I intended or why. I guess I expected some qualifying questions or a referral, but not anger and abuse. I was not in a very pleasant state of mind myself.

"What am I supposed to do for justice, shoot the sheriff in the fucking guts!" It wasn't the smartest thing to say; she hung up and so did I. Cassie came into the room and suggested we go visit mother and tell her about our great vacation. That sounded good to me, and the drive and visit was a treat for us both. We started our return in relaxed and upbeat moods. At the corner of Center Hill Road and Church Street I noticed a sheriff's car racing up behind us, lights flashing.

I pulled over and stopped. In no time, Sheriff Bertram jumped out of the cruiser along with Walter Shook and the under sheriff, all brandishing guns that they shoved through the open windows of our little Mazda truck. Cassie was terrified. Bertram shouted at me to get out of the truck, and when I stood in front of him he screamed in my face.

"Do you know who I am? Do you know who I am?"

I was scared and baffled at the same time. "You're Sheriff Bertram," I managed.

"You called the Bar Association in Albany and threatened to shoot me! Do you know who I am? Do you know who I am?"

It wasn't an easy moment, but I tried to explain the call and the fact that I was referring to Sheriff Proper who had arrested my son and I was trying to get a referral for a lawyer. Bertram quieted down a bit. Investigator Shook was silent, but I am not sure he lowered his gun yet. I thought later that he knew that Frank had not been the fire starter and just stood there silently. He never told the new sheriff even as the fires went on. Then Bertram threatened me.

"You've been writing letters to the paper," he said. "If you write any more letters to the editor, I'll ruin you. I'll get Judge Munson's decision and publish it!"

Bertram told me the bar association had my call on tape and made sure I got the message. It was an extremely unsettling incident for both Cassie and me. She was sure that if she had not been there, they would have hauled me into custody and beaten me bloody. She was shaken by the incident and forbid me from doing anything further about the case.

NEW ROAD BYPASSES TOWN AND TIME

Before the new road bypassed downtown Copake, Route 22 carried a steady stream of travelers along Main Street through the center of town, and the dining room at the Holsapple House was always busy with overnight guests. Other businesses flourished, too.

Just past Dean's dairy barn, the firehouse anchored a lot of town activity in its upstairs meeting rooms. Up the street, Fred Link built his frozen food locker and sold appliances. Rounding the sharp corner, you came to Folger's auction house, and across the street, Pete Miles set up his lumber business in Wally Funk's old cow barn. Route 22 continued winding through the bustling hamlet of Copake Falls on the edge of the state park.

Copake Falls was the redoubt of Foster Ham, taxi man. Foster kept a busy summer schedule meeting one or another of the five express trains that ran on the Harlem division of the New York Central railroad from New York City. When the new road bypassed Boston Corners, Copake and Copake Falls, it took the train ten years to follow suit. The advent of the Taconic Parkway to the west of town siphoned off most of the remaining traffic, and the effects on local businesses could be seen and felt.

The changes were most visible at the Holsapple House where Ray Burch had always worn his white bartender coat and where a waitress had traditionally hand wrung a bell to announce dinner from the bottom of the stairs. With the drop of business, the Holsapple House had trouble keeping good chefs and the food and service became merely ordinary. Along with the rest of Copake, the Holsapple House declined into rusticity.

The law is good if a man use it legally.
—The first epistle of Paul the Apostle to Timothy

The story of my demise, I guess you could call it, was a nightmare of the court's legal maneuvers. The fires were bad, but in the end the lawyers did more damage than the arsonist. This was hard because I believe in the integrity of the courts. Some people will claim I brought it upon myself, but I was raised to believe in the Constitution; I believe that state and local governments are bound to its principles of fair trials and equal protection. Our Constitution binds the government to the people and not the people to the government. Our Constitution is the law of the land.

Something is wrong in Copake. It is not only wrong in Copake but in Columbia County and beyond into the Federal Courts. The courts left my son to be tried by the rumor of the law and the tale of the street. That is because he never got a trial that established his innocence. It seems remarkable, but he was arrested for a major crime and never had a chance to testify in his own defense, even in Federal District Court when we tried to recover damages. That led to the conclusion of his guilt. In hiring lawyers and trying to help his defense, I'm sure I made errors, but I was trying to do the right thing. The representation I found in the legal system was often incompetent, and parts of it were even corrupt. The courts, the place I call "Club Justice," seemed to favor the police at every turn. There, judges and lawyers seem to rush to a presumption of guilt in support of our protectors, the police. Stonewalled and disenfranchised, I no longer hold a benefit of the doubt in my attitude toward the lawyers or the courts. It is extremely difficult for me to reconstruct the events of the legal proceedings that ruined my family's life in Copake, but I will try. After all, with a heritage tied to this land for over three centuries, I still hold loyalties to the ideals of the land of the free and the home of the brave. And, frankly, I dearly miss those beliefs I used to take for granted.

When the Columbia County sheriff arrested Frank for starting the fire at Bull Spring Farm, he did not read him his Miranda rights. In addition, the confession he signed was not authored by him, nor was it a document of the truth. It was a forced confession backed only by facts pulled out of midair that bore no resemblance to what happened. He was intimidated and frightened, and although we all wish Frank had not signed the damned thing, the malicious intent of the sheriff's office and the skullduggery that took advantage of Frank's weaknesses should condemn the actions of the law enforcers.

The charges they made were never intended to be heard in Court. From the arrest, the subsequent arraignment hearing with all the news coverage, the stage was set for my plunge into the system I call Club Justice. Catching the real arsonist, clearing Frank's name and reputation, and recovering my own damages in paying lawyers fees became the interlocking horns of my dilemma. The farm, the family, and the town were at stake as far as I was concerned. Engaging in the legal system I had believed in all my life turned out to be my inglorious undoing. Mad as hell about it all, I'm still writing letters and making phone calls to judges who figured I'd go away.

The loss of my farm and the dissolution of my family in Copake resonate with my disillusionment with the legal system and in particular with the attorneys I retained and judges who administered the law. Like most people who decide they need legal representation, I relied on the services of my parents' lawyer and continued on from there along the route of references and referrals. Judge Robert Myers had done legal work for my mother, so I first went to him for guidance. Tom Griffen worked out of Myers's firm at first, and then as Myers cut back, Griffen and Carl Whitbeck, another young lawyer, joined the Rapport firm. Jason Shaw came along later, and that's how I came to rely on them for legal representation and counsel.

The only trouble was that the firm soon became attorneys for the county. That would not work well for my case, obviously, as a plaintiff against the county. Conflict of interest would be a concern. My accountant recommended a firm in New York City, Cohen and Adolph. That was December 1987, and instead of getting the straightforward direction from the big city attorneys I had anticipated, things just got more complicated. Cohen told me he could not take the criminal case, but would do the civil case.

MY WORST CHRISTMAS, AND AN UNHAPPY NEW YEAR

I never spent a worse Christmas. First, I was told my son's trial would begin before Christmas, so I thought things would be cleared up by the holidays. But, a new DA would be taking over and that caused a delay. Frank and I met with our lawyer and the fire investigator right after the New Year. We went over the facts that were known about the fire and we were ready for the trial.

On January 3, the County Board of Supervisors met to approve the newly appointed County Attorney, none other than Carl Whitbeck of the firm representing our case with the county. I sat in the back of the room and worried about the conflict of interest question. When Whitbeck took the stand to testify and was asked about any possible conflict of interest with the new job, he could only "think of one." It happened to be his representation of the Germantown landfill, and he claimed another firm was taking that representation. That was it. Whitbeck was approved for County Attorney.

I was steamed, but helpless to do anything about it. Now, the County Attorneys was also supposed to be defending Frank. After the adjournment of the hearing, I greeted Carl Whitbeck as he worked his way to the back of the room. He was obviously embarrassed, and felt the need to explain he "wanted to do something for the County." It was a duty and privilege, he said. Any thought of a conflict of interest in our case didn't get mentioned. Despite my frustration I hoped all would end for the best.

The trial was going to take place in the Hudson. Hudson was founded by a group of New England businessmen involved in the whale oil business around 1810. The main business street, Warren Street, starts at the Hudson River and went up the grade east. The street on one side catered to the returning seaman with bars, gambling and prostitution, while the other side had many fine old homes. The whale oil business was very profitable right up until the introduction of kerosene for lighting. After that, the ropewalk, used to manufacture rope for the sailing ships, burned and wasn't rebuilt, and the ships gradually left. Then Hudson started a long decline with the one part of town maintaining the bawdy character that Hudson became known for. A slow recovery with cement manufacturing leading the way seemed to end with the closing of the cement plants. The Columbia County Courthouse, reflecting the slow economy, seemed stalled in time. It stands in a park on Union Street among law offices and some fine old homes, typical of many rural counties. It was built about 1910 with steps leading up to the marble entry and its offices and record vaults on the first floor. A large marble staircase leads up to the courtrooms on the second floor.

It was January 11, 1988. It was frigid outside and the old-fashioned courtroom felt cold and looked cold, too, with its industrial style windows competing with the atmosphere intended by the marble trim and oil paintings along the walls. Judge John G. Leaman entered and took his place at the bench as we all stood. He wasted little time in calling for heat. The bailiff placed a call to the boiler room and in no time the pipes clanged and hissed with steam heat. It was a relief for everyone. We were small in number, but full of purpose.

We were there to determine the reliability of the statement Frank signed and to see if it could be admitted as evidence. If a trial were appropriate, it would begin directly following the hearing. The statement was the only evidence the State had; they didn't have a motive. Although it had been alleged that Frank was a pyromaniac, examination by the State psychiatrist agreed with the two examinations we obtained, so pyromania was ruled out as motive. If Judge Leaman ruled against the use of the signed statement as evidence, the case could be resolved right there. No trial necessary.

Seven witnesses would be called. Our lawyer, Jason Shaw, decided that witnesses would not be allowed to hear each other's testimonies, except for Frank because he was the one being charged with a crime. Judge Leaman called the lawyers to the bench where the DA, Paul Czajka tried to limit the scope of the hearing to whether the statement was voluntary or not. The judge ruled that the inquiry extended to other questions as well: whether the statement was gained by custodial interrogation, whether Miranda rights were given in timely fashion, whether the right to counsel was violated. For Shaw, it was like winning round one.

The first witness, David Proper, took the stand, and I was shown to the hallway through the door near the front of the courtroom. Wilson, Cozzolino and Morgan, all from the opposing side, were directed out the back door to the long corridor outside. The sheriff had been excused from the hearing by the judge, so as to not interfere with his duties, and the procedure continued. From the court transcript, the order and nature of the hearing can be clearly summarized, and I have focused on the details that apply most directly to the issues and actions closest to effecting Frank's innocence or guilt.

David Proper described an investigation of underage beer sales and how he and Deputy Wilson picked up his friend, Frank Langdon, and procured a statement at the town hall. Then Proper recounted how he and Wilson took Frank Langdon on a ten-mile ride while they asked questions about the fire. Proper claimed Frank Langdon offered to help and went along on the ride voluntarily. After Frank was driven to Hillsdale, Frank seemed to want to get something off his chest, he testified. Questions about the fire continued. Apparently, the deputies suspected then that Frank had something to do with the fire.

He testified that the next day, July 21, 1987, the two men returned and asked Frank to go with them to identify the sales clerk at Stewart's. Under oath, David Proper admitted taking Frank Langdon to the sheriff's office, where he knew Frank would be interrogated about the fire by a couple of experts. The testimony explains how Investigator Cozzolino took Frank to the sheriff's office for questioning, that Frank was told he could leave anytime, and that he was not under arrest. Then, David Proper, Frank's ride, was sent away.

The questioning continued and Frank became agitated. David Proper was then asked to come back into the interrogation room where he ostensibly offered his help and friendship to Frank, who was still struggling to "get it off his chest." David Proper recounted how Cozzolino asked how the fire had started, and that Frank responded with the cigarette story. Mainly, after he had finished milking the cows, Frank said he flipped a cigarette into the haymow intending to start a fire and burn the barn. Frank was also questioned about the 1985 barn fire, and he admitted to turning a light on, very close to some wood, spider

webs and dust. That caused that fire. Proper then described
Frank's reading and signing of the statement.

Czajka then asked about lunch, apparently to establish the
fact that Frank was provided with lunch by the sheriff's office.
Then the DA presented the signed statement. David Proper was
asked when Frank was arrested, and he responded that it was
after the description of the 1985 fire. Czajka introduced the fact
that Frank was a non-smoker, anticipating that issue as a defense
to be brought up later.

Jason Shaw's cross-examination drew out much more detail. He said that Deputy Wilson had taken notes at the Hillsdale
questioning, but that he had not been given copies. He also asked
if David and Frank drank beer together as members of the fire
company. David couldn't remember serving Frank after the Bristol fire in the presence of a Mr. Miller. This was David's claim
even though he served beer regularly at the fire house. It appears
Sheriff Proper wasn't very concerned about underage drinking.
His son was serving minors at the fire house. As a former fire
chief and regular at the fire house, Sheriff Proper must have
known about it.

Shaw picked up the questioning by focusing on the day of
the arrest. Shaw established that the paperwork was kept in
David Proper's truck. Then he asked why, instead of filling it out
in the truck, they took Frank to the town hall to fill out a form.
David Proper admitted that they planned to take Frank to Hillsdale to question him about the fire all along. At some point during the trip they accused him of starting the fire. In response to
questioning David described Frank as being upset, on the verge
of tears.

That is when Judge Leaman broke in. He asked David if Miranda rights had been given at any time during the day, David
Proper told the judge they had not.

Shaw continued with the questioning. David said they
dropped Frank off and then returned to the sheriff's office to
meet with Cozzolino and Morgan. After a discussion of the ses-
sion with Frank, they made plans to take Frank to the sheriff's office the next day for more intensive interrogation.

Shaw's questioning continued. He got David Proper to re-
late the sequence of getting Frank, going to Stewart's, and then
stopping at the sheriff's office. David claimed to have checked the

logbook for a call he had made at Stewart's but he said later he didn't know if it had been logged or not. He also claimed that Frank had gone into the store and that he and Wilson had followed. Frank told me they had taken him directly to the sheriff's office without stopping at Stewart's.

David Proper testified that Frank was asked to write a description of the girl and then Frank was given a tour of the communications room. Frank was then taken to the office by Cozzolino and Morgan and told that he was not under arrest and that he was free to leave. In response to Shaw's questioning David said he and deputy Wilson were then sent to get Frank something to eat. They returned with the food, but turned it over to the sheriff and were sent back out. It wasn't long afterwards that David was called in to help with the interrogation.

From Frank's description of the incident to me it became clear that Cozzolino and Morgan played the roles of "bad" cops. Cozzolino pounded the desk and yelled in Frank's face. "Be a fucking man! Admit you did it!" Sheriff Proper must have been poised in the hall on the other side of the open door. He was directing things and he decided he wanted David to be the "good" cop. His testimony indicated he was certainly ready and willing to play that part. This was his first investigation, and he was a star already.

Under Shaw's questioning David Proper described how Frank seemed to want to get something off his chest. He said he held Frank's arm and asked him to tell the truth because he wanted to help him as a friend.

At that point the DA was apparently concerned about the reading of Miranda rights. He broke into the hearing. He asked if David's testimony were correct. David answered in the affirmative. Then an off-the-record discussion was held with the judge. The rookie and the seasoned police investigator had not given a Miranda warning to Frank. That much was clear from the record. The judge decided to break for lunch.

When the hearing continued, Miranda seemed to be the focus of the questioning. Shaw established in questioning David Proper that Frank had appeared to be on the edge of telling something, and he (D. Proper) had urged him to confess. At that point, David testified Cozzolino left the room. Shaw continued with a rapid line of questions. Was Frank asked if he wanted to go home? Did he want to call his father? Was Frank informed of his rights to remain silent, to secure an attorney? Was Frank told that anything he said could be used against him in a court of law? David Proper answered "NO" to each question.

According to David's testimony, Frank was still distressed and on the brink of breaking down when Cozzolino returned to the room. Even then, he was not read his rights. The pressure was continued for a confession of guilt by David, who held Frank's arm and claimed he was there to help and by Cozzolino's table pounding. According to David Proper's statement, Frank said he threw a cigarette up into the hay to start the fire. They also got him to say he had turned on the light that ignited the 1985 barn fire. It was only then, Cozzolino read Frank his rights. David testified that since Frank refused to write out the statement, Cozzolino did. Then Morgan entered and continued questioning Frank.

It was about this time in the day that I called and got Frank on the phone. He could barely speak. Shortly after that, Tom Griffin called the sheriff's office and stopped the questioning.

The next witness, Deputy Wilson, was questioned by DA Czajka, and testimony recounting how Frank was picked up on July 20, taken to the town hall where he gave a deposition, driven to Hillsdale and delivered home was given. Wilson also verified the course of the next days' events. Then, Shaw cross-examined.

Shaw asked for the notes that Wilson had taken on July 20, and the Judge called a recess to give Wilson time to find the notes. The notes were not found. The hearing resumed. Judge Leaman questioned Wilson about the whereabouts of the notes. Wilson said he had turned them in along with his other paperwork.

Investigator Cozzolino was sent to search the sheriff's office for the notes, and after Czajka and Shaw talked with him about the search, the judge called for a recess until the next day, January 12, 1988.

On the 12th Deputy Wilson returned with the notes. He was sworn in again and Czajka resumed with questioning on how the notes were found. While these notes were printed on the back of a form, his other notes were scribbled in a notebook. Wilson said the notes were found in another file that was in his bedroom. Czajka presented the notes and they were then put into evidence. The lawyers gathered around the bench for a short conversation.

A short recess was called and Shaw came out into the hall to show me the notes. They were printed clearly as questions and answers on the back of a form, not in script on a pocket note-book page like the other notes. The paper was folded a number of times as if it were placed in a shirt pocket. Shaw said both he and Czajka believed the notes had been written the night before and not at the time of the investigation in July. The unanswered question for me was what did the real notes say and why did they disappear? Did they include directions from the sheriff himself to waive a Miranda warning?

On Shaw's cross-examination of Wilson, he asked why the notes were so different in comparison to the others. He asked for the original notebook from the DA's file. There were four pages, no fifth page, and Wilson maintained his claim that they were the only notes and that was how he found them.

Shaw's questioning was then interrupted, and the lawyers had another off-the-record conversation with the judge. After the discussion, the notes were referred to as the "alleged notes." Despite the doubts of the lawyers and the judge, Wilson stood his ground. The notes along with the notebook were entered into evidence. Shaw then established that Wilson had not filed a supplemental report form, which was the usual procedure. Czajka broke in again and asked to approach the bench. After a short off-the-record discussion, the hearing took another direction.

Shaw asked Wilson about a conversation the sheriff had with me about arranging a polygraph test that Frank had agreed to take but that was never given. Shaw established Wilson's movements the night of the fire, including his visit to the house with Shook and Kane later that night. Wilson stated that he talked to Frank the night of the fire, and that Frank said he drank some beer while milking. Wilson said he considered Frank a suspect. The fact that I had named a suspect in the fire did not get mentioned, nor was Shook's odd reaction mentioned.

Then Shaw had Wilson recount what happened when he and David Proper picked up Frank on July 20, and he asked how the notes had been taken. Shaw again established the fact that no Miranda warning was given.

Judge Leaman broke in and asked whether either Frank or I had been informed that Frank would be questioned about the fire. Wilson said we were not informed.

Shaw went on to confirm David Proper's testimony about leaving Frank with Cozzolino and Morgan at the sheriff's office. Shaw finished, and since Czajka had no further questions, court broke for lunch. I was given scant information about what went on and Frank and I went for lunch. It gave me time to sort of measure the situation. The fact that no Miranda warning was given ruled out the use of the prosecution's one piece of evidence. That was without getting into the issue of custodial interrogation, the lost notes and the missing report. Then, there was the signed statement. Why would someone who didn't smoke start a fire with a cigarette? The state psychiatrist had established that Frank was not a pyromaniac. So, there was no motive.

At 1:30 P.M. sharp the hearing was called to order. Immediately Czajka addressed the court. He requested an adjournment stating, "Information has come to my attention that could potentially affect the outcome of the suppression hearing and ultimately the indictment itself." Frank and I headed back to the farm in a somewhat up-beat mood but, because of all the off-the-record discussions at the bench, a little in the dark about what was going on.

I think it was about 4:30 that afternoon when the phone rang; I was in the kitchen. It was Jason Shaw. His voice was animated and he had really dramatic news. He asked if I remembered a note investigator Shook made that described Arthur Coleman, Jr. smelling burned flesh as he drove past a truck on Snyder Pond Road on the night of the fire. I did remember it, but at the time it had seemed too bazaar to be true. How could anyone smell burned flesh just by passing a truck? Anyway I didn't see how anyone could have gotten away from Bull Spring without being seen. With so much chaos at the time we decided to look into the matter later.

Shaw kept talking. He said that after court he and Czajka went to Czajka's office to call Shook on the speakerphone. Shook verified the investigation of the "man with burned flesh." Coleman had indeed passed the man and smelled burned flesh. But it was right on a very sharp curve on Snyder Pond road. Because of the curve both vehicles had to go very slow. That's how Coleman could see the man who was burned, and because the windows were down, how he could smell the flesh. Shook said that the only way the man could have been in that place in that condition was if he had gotten burned when he started the fire. Cole-man described a late model blue Toyota with a long bed and white cap. Shook reported that he had gone to the hospitals in the area and checked with police in Edgemont trying to locate burn victims. Unfortunately, Shook was unable to identify the man. I hung up the phone in disbelief. It was a mystery to me how anyone could have escaped without being spotted, at least by the Lilly family.

The next morning Frank and I arrived at the courthouse. I expected to take up my position in the hall, while the lawyers continued inside. Instead, we were shown to the judge's chambers. Czajka said he wanted to make a brief application to give Shaw a chance to review the matters of the past few days and prepare a memorandum of law on the facts so far presented. He said it could promote judicial economy and avoid further testimony. Judge Leaman asked Shaw what line of inquiry he was going to pursue and also what he had to say to Czajka's proposal. Shaw launched into a dissertation about cases concerning custodial interrogation. Leaman seemed skeptical but said he had no problem with a modest recess. Then Czajka asked for another private conference, and Frank and I were sent to the hall. When Frank and I returned, a recess was announced until Friday afternoon.

When court reconvened, DA Czajka made a brief statement about the review he had made of testimony by expert witnesses, grand jury notes and statements of evidence. "I would note for the record that in making these reviews I found no fault in the action of my predecessor, nor do I place any blame with the investigating agencies. It's been my decision to make and mine alone, and I would ask the Court note that for the record."

Shaw's answering comment at the invitation of the judge followed. "Your honor, I obviously would join in the motion. I would like to, on the record, commend Mr. Czajka for his interest in seeing that justice is done and his desire in the case to take it upon himself to do justice." With that, Judge Leaman dismissed the indictment "by reason of the determination not to go forward with it." Then he commended the two lawyers.

A few days before this, I had been in the hall when I asked Shaw how much more money it was going to cost. I had no idea where I would come up with additional money beyond the $30,000 already spent. He told me another $50,000 would do it.

And, the way this hearing had turned out, ending without going to trial, Shaw said he could call it a win. Shaw assured me the volation of Frank's civil rights was very flagrant. In a civil case I could pursue the violation of Frank's civil rights and a lawyer could take the case on contingency. Both Shaw and Tom Griffin assured me that Frank's civil rights had been violated in a big way. What hadn't come out in the hearing would come out in civil court. Moving ahead in civil court, given my cash poor situation, seemed like the best option.

What I hoped for was that Frank would get his day in court, eventually. What hadn't come out in the hearing would get aired in a civil case and establish Frank's innocence, not just the fact that an investigation was flawed and led to no indictment.

PURSUING JUSTICE: COMPLICATIONS, AGGRAVATION

Because of the assurance that Frank's civil rights had been so grossly violated, it seemed reasonable that obtaining damages for a false arrest case would not be a problem. I proceeded with the civil case. Thanks to Ralph Fuentes, we had evidence on how the fire started, and we also knew Shook had not investigated the man I identified as a suspect in the fire. We also knew that Shook already established the burned man seen by Arthur J. Coleman as the one who started the fire when Frank was arrested. In my opinion, all the other evidence pointed to the probability that the sheriff knew the identity of the man who was burning my barns. In the sworn testimony before Judge Leaman it was established that Frank's civil rights were violated. It seemed a slam dunk.

Of course, it wasn't that simple. After the firm of Cohen and Adolph got the case it dragged on for the rest of the year. The first hold-up was they had to wait several months for the transcript of the hearing. Even after they got the notes they had no idea what was said in all those off-the-record discussions. Critical notes were "lost" or misplaced. Then a big blow came when Cohen and Adolph got evicted from their offices in Manhattan.

When District Attorney, Paul Czajka, opted out of the case before a decision was made it left a lot of unanswered questions. It seemed to me Czajka didn't want them answered. I fault him for that because I believed he could have found out who was setting the fires and had him arrested. One account indicated that the arsonist was destroying a million dollars worth of building each year. To me it seemed he was up to his neck in a cover-up. He did not even inform his own investigator, who was independent of the sheriff's office, about what he knew about the fires. He did not tell his investigator about what he learned from Walter Shook. His investigator, and others on the case, went blindly forward, continuing to go after their chosen culprit, Frank. I knew a suit against the police would not be popular, but it seemed like I was in the middle of a war. Instead of the investigators and lawyers making order and sense, things got more chaotic.

Back in New York, Adolph kept asking me about a specific tape that was supposed to be in the file. I'd transferred the file that contained several tapes from Shaw and told him Shaw said everything was in the file. I told him to look again. What I did not know was that the tape that Adolph was looking for, our tape showing in trial after trial that a cigarette would not start a fire was not there. The edited home video Morgan made showing a cigarette starting a fire was in the file. It appeared Adolph did not have a reason to believe what I was saying. He may have even doubted that we actually made the tape! Another thing, there were no notes or even an indication that two examinations had found that Frank was not a pyromaniac in the file.

Adolph kept insinuating that my case was frivolous. I had to approach ballistic levels just in order to get him to file the case. There is no doubt in my mind the missing tape created the problem. Depositions, the lawyers stock and trade, were not being done, and Cohen was as good at excuses as the opposing lawyers. In frustration, I started to go to other lawyers hoping they would help move my case. I paid a lawyer named Gagen $500, and he gladly took the money and gave two cents worth of advice. Cassie and I went to several more lawyers and finally wound up at the Wilcox firm in Troy. They refused to take the case at that late date, but I did learn the statute of limitations was almost up. After that the case could not be refiled. A previous lawyer was wrong when he told me no statute of limitations existed in police matters.

Finally, Steven Cohen told me the other side moved for Summary Judgment. I understood that to mean the court would be going directly to the damages phase because they admitted that Frank's civil rights had been violated. Both Shaw and Griffin had said the violations were "bad" and that was even without the news of Shook's investigation. But this was not the case.

We went into the courtroom and sat down. Federal District Judge Howard G. Munson of the Northern District of New Your entered. I felt uneasy and perhaps a little mystified with Judge Munson's comments on the way to the bench. He said, "I don't know why they sent me this case, it belongs back in Columbia County." I mentioned this in a conversation with Judge Myers later, and it stumped him too because he thought that the case was exactly where it belonged-in Judge Munson's court. Or, it could have gone to an Albany judge that, in Myers words, "wasn't doing anything." Later I learned Resila, the opposing lawyer, clerked for the Albany judge. Anyway, presentations were made, and I thought Adolph did well. He seemed to present a good case that Miranda rights were not given from what came out in the Leaman hearing

Attorney James A. Resila of the firm of Carter, Conboy, Case Blackmore, Maloney & Laird in Albany presented for the other side. What he said didn't impress me much but he claimed the arrest was proper and there was no cause for action. Then he presented affidavits from those involved, the sheriff and his deputies. They all claiming Frank was told the door was open, given Miranda rights, and told he could leave and so forth. Technically, I suppose the door was open, and yes after a while he was read his rights, but if was far from a legal arrest as was shown in the Leaman hearing. By claiming the arrest was proper when it was not proper I believe Resila lied and that he knew it. I believe he was very familiar with what his clients said at the Leaman hearing.

By the end of Resila's presentation, I was boiling mad and Adolph had to restrain me. Outside the courtroom, Adolph introduced me to Resila; I guess I was still mad and it showed. I stepped forward and said straight out, "You lied!" "I'm sorry, I'm sorry," he said. He backed up several steps before he turned and scurried down the hall. I later likened his reaction to that of a cockroach when a light is turned on. That is exactly what it reminded me of.

Judge Munson was going to hand down his decision from the bench in Albany. When the decision was reported to have been made, I headed to meet Adolph at the train station so we could drive to the courthouse together, but at the last minute I was paged and informed that the train had broken down. Adolph would not be meeting me at the station and the decision would be handed down the next month. I decided to proceed to the courthouse on my own. Once there, I watched Judge Munson hand down three decisions, all involving the police in some way. One I distinctly remember because of a young woman weeping just two benches behind me. The judge ruled in that case that the City of Saratoga Springs couldn't fire a female officer for her refusal to carry a gun, but instead had to provide her with a desk job. I also remember being impressed with Judge Munson's care and concern in his decisions on these cases. It appeared all sides were given a chance to be heard and the system did indeed work.

It was another month before Adolph and I attended a nearly empty courtroom. Judge Munson entered, sat down, looked around and said, "Well, here we go." An auspicious beginning, I thought, and then he asked if anyone had anything to add. The lawyers declined. Judge Munson seemed to grin and swung his head all the way to the left. Then he swung it to the right saying, "all right!" Looking back, I call that his "now I got you." moment. It raised a little apprehension in me. Adolph relied on testimony from David Proper and Wilson from the Leaman hearing in his papers showing a violation.

Judge Munson started out denying Adolph's plea for a hearing on the constitutionality of the confession. With no hearing Frank was not going to have a chance to testify. If that didn't concern me enough, the judge continued to cite case after case in which an affidavit of someone present at the arrest was needed to overcome a summary judgment motion. Then he pointed out that Adolph had not presented such an affidavit. Then, Judge Munson ruled that the existence of the confession established grounds for a legal arrest, and further, that the arrest was proper. "This is final," he concluded. He adjourned the court.

That did it for me. I pushed past my lawyer to address the court. The stenographer strained to take it all down. I pointed out that Sheriff Proper was trying to shut me up, and it was at the point of costing me the farm. I told them about the burned man and the fact I named a suspect. Judge Munson then broke in and asked Adolph to inform me of the limitations of Federal Court. I again addressed the court and asked how we get justice in these United States? Judge Munson cut me off and asked Adolph to explain, with regard to the Bar Association procedures, and so forth. Adolph apologized to the judge. Judge Munson accepted the apology, but I didn't miss the implication that if I didn't like his decision, I could sue my lawyer.

Article 7 of the Bill of Rights guarantees trial by jury in civil cases for anything valued at more than $20. I spent $30,000 in legal fees to defend my son against charges the sheriff knew were untrue. My son was branded in the community as "the Copake Arsonist" and his ability to one day take over the farm or even live in the community was in doubt. Indeed, the very ownership of the farm and the ability to live in the community was destroyed not just for my son but for me as well. My son never got to testify on his own behalf, and he never got to face his accuser in court. Judge Munson, not a jury as stipulated under Article 7 of the Constitution, denied damages. He protected the sheriff and allowed the arsonist to remain at large! I knew in my guts that his decision would ruin my son and cost me my farm.

It took a half an hour before I could drive Adolph back to the train. When I got home I wrote Judge Munson about my problems with Adolph and Cohen. When Cohen learned of the letter, he resigned. Perhaps he could see no future in the case for them. For me, I had no alternative. I had to find another lawyer to file an appeal before time ran out.

I was still fueled by the hope of getting things right. I followed the advice of a close friend and secured the services of a "good, aggressive" lawyer, Gary Greenwald. After a meeting with him in Middletown, it was established that he would do an appeal for $7,000 (up front). Because time was running out, Frank and I sold our young livestock, and I worked a deal with Ben Ackley involving land adjoining his farm so we could pay Greenwald. He thought Frank would make a good impression on the court. He also encouraged me by saying he read the Munson decision and proclaiming we had gotten "screwed." But he also said that the lack of an affidavit was the only reason we lost and that there wasn't anything else Munson could have done. I scoffed at that. He didn't even give Frank a chance to testify. When I left, I believed an appeal would be made. The decision was wrong. Greenwald filed the appeal August 5 in plenty of time.

At a later meeting it appeared Greenwald had been to the Court of Appeals in New York. He said that because the decision had been made final, the affidavit could not be included in an appeal, and we would lose in the Court of Appeals. It appeared to me that the appeals judge was more interested in whether the rules of the court were followed than what actually happened. Perhaps he also failed to notice that Frank was never able to testify on his own behalf. Anyway, Greenwald was up against Resila, who specialized in defending municipalities. Greenwald's solution was to win a 60–a motion, claiming problems with the lawyers. The Court of Appeals, rather than denying the appeal right there, allowed a stipulation sending it back to Judge Munson's court. He had just 30 days from Judge Munson's decision to get the appeal reinstated. He promised he could get us back into Munson's court.

There was certainly a long list of lawyer problems. First was the conflict of interest when the Rapport firm became county attorneys. Then there was the problem with Adolph that sent me to lawyer after lawyer looking for help. Resila even complained about them and Judge Munson knew they resigned. But on September 17, Greenwald signed the stipulation. After he signed that, the only recourse was the number 60 motion in Munson's court or to reinstate the appeal that the Court of Appeals seemed unwilling to grant anyway, within the time limit.

Greenwald's paralegal had Frank and me sign an affidavit, and we moved forward in the belief that Greenwald would get us back in court. The presentation was made and Judge Munson announced he would make a decision in a letter to the lawyer before Christmas. I would not receive a copy. This was no small cause for more worry. In other motions and decisions I received a copy as well as the lawyer.

Just before Christmas I started calling Greenwald's office for the decision, and I was told that it wasn't in yet. I continued calling three or four times a week and was told the same each time; the decision is not in yet. Two months had passed when I went to the post office to find a letter from Greenwald. On the way back to the house I opened it to read the decision. The motion was denied. It was dated December 7, and now it was well past the 60 days when the case could be reargued and well past the 30 days to get the appeal reinstated! So, it appeared to me Greenwald, the aggressive lawyer who would help me address the failures of my previous lawyers, failed to come clean with me. It appeared he took my money and ruined any chance reargue or to appeal Judge Munson's decision.

In reviewing Greenwald's papers it appeared he covered all bases and Judge Munson's decision seemed arbitrary. A question in my mind to this day is, did Gary Greenwald just not want to deal with it anymore? Was there ever a chance of wining in the Court of Appeals? When Resila agreed to the stipulation was it just a face saving gesture for Greenwald? Could the appeal been reinstated could it be won in the Court of Appeals? Perhaps not.

We live in a law and order society; one that believes that, as lawyer Shaw said, "the police have to have some leeway or they can't do their job." Another question is, what do you do when the police do not do their job? My son, arrested for a major crime, never got a chance to testify or face his accuser, and no jury was ever involved; only judges. The person that burned my barns went free. I doubted the decision was really misplaced to only show up 60 days later.

The decision to file suit against the police in the first place was not an easy one. I was at the post office one day and a neighbor said, "Everyone wants to sue and get rich." I knew there would be people that would take that attitude, yet the damages were real. Suing the police also made the police an enemy. I was not prepared that the damages would be so great. The night Frank's Garage burned State Fire Investigator Morgan, who was in on the arrest, called me over to the porch of the Holsapple House and demanded I drop the suit against the Sheriff and his deputies. He gave what I took as a veiled threat when he said "your son will wind up at one of these fires with a bullet in his back. That led to me calling my lawyer at 2 a.m. and a meeting with the led investigator Vick and Deputy Harrison on one side, and Steve Cohen, Frank and myself on the other. There was no doubt the police went into the meeting believing Frank might have set the fire. Fortunately Frank was at a Kenny Rogers Concert and had the tickets to prove it.

What impressed me was how little the man in charge of the arson investigations knew, like the fact I named a suspect the night of the Bull Spring Fire. He also didn't know about the burned man and Shook's investigation. We recorded the meeting on tape and a complaint about Morgan's statement was filed with the State. Morgan lost his job after that.

P.S. I still have the tape.

FOUND GUILTY WITHOUT TRIAL

Judge Munson's decision that Frank's arrest was proper devastated me. The next morning I went to Frank Stang's Garage for coffee and Butch Near was there. Butch was the third ranking politician in the county as majority leader to the County Board of Supervisors. His position would be roughly equivalent to a County Commissioner where there is a Board of Commissioners. Butch was already talking about the decision. It was a great relief to him that the court had found the arrest of my son proper. "Yes sir that shows Paul followed the law," he said. "He did everything right, Frankie did the fire."

Mad as hell, I objected. I even explained in detail how the fire had started, but with the judge's decision figuratively in hand, Butch held firm. I stormed out, determined to clear my son's name, and back at A.D.'s desk I drafted "As to How the Fire Started." I based it on the facts we had gathered for the trial that never happened. I took it to the local paper, but they refused to print it. They said they were too small to do all the investigations needed to satisfy their lawyer. They didn't want to get sued, and of course they did a lot of business with the county. I made copies and handed them out to any individuals willing to take a look, but I felt I was spinning my wheels. With the arson fires continuing and Frank taking the brunt of suspicion, the pressure continued to mount. Frank was looked upon as a sort of leper, and it wasn't long before he pack up and left for what he hoped would be a better opportunity in western New York.

LOSING GROUND

With the arson fires continuing, Frank continued to take the brunt of suspicion, and it simply became too much for him. I remember how sad I was the day he departed for the western part of the state. He hoped to outdistance the cruel scrutiny of Copake and make a new future for himself.

Not ten minutes after Frank left, I was back in my office and the church carillon chimed the wedding march, and I slumped into a deep depression as my losses hit home. It was okay with me that Frank took his cows along with his hopes, but he would never marry in the church of my family's heritage, and the town's people would never be there to celebrate. I lamented my daughter's situation in Rochester where she was working her way through RIT, and my other son Cliff's imminent departure for service in Korea increased my longing for better times. About a half hour later there was someone at the door. They were from the fire company and they said that they heard Frank was gone and they wanted the fire radio.

With fewer cows and the other business problems, it was clear I was facing a cash flow deficit. The bank demanded repayment of the funds loaned for the house moves. I managed to get a second mortgage to pay the note, but I couldn't secure additional funds. I was forced to ask for interest only payments until spring, but they refused, in spite of my stellar record of no missed payments. They told me if I missed a payment they would foreclose. With Cassie carrying the burden, we got into a Chapter 11 bankruptcy for reorganization. The plan was to sell the two houses, now moved, and pay the mortgage down.

I worked hard to sell the houses, but the bankruptcy seemed to stymie the market and potential buyers didn't want to get involved. Eventually, I managed to make some progress, but, of course, there was a catch. A buyer for the blue house turned up, but the deal had to be closed by the end of the tax year. And, I needed to add more land to the deal. The bank went along with the subdivision but was noncommittal on the reorganization. Delays on the subdivision held up the approval until the end of the year, but it appeared that the house would be sold under the judge's approval and that we would be able to end the bankruptcy protection.

Cassie and I were happy going to court for the very first time. The house would be sold and we could end Chapter 11. Guess again. Production Credit and Victor Myers showed up for the first time. Our motion to sell the house was read, but Myers objected. He claimed the bank should get money too, not just to pay the first mortgage. The judge didn't know what to do with the new set of circumstances and he delayed the sale until a future meeting. The buyer sent a letter of withdrawal from the sale offer because he would be extended beyond the end of the year, which wouldn't worked for his purposes. That did it for me. I was left without a plan.

Things were so bad at the farm that I let the referee's decision to end protection stand and I surrendered. Waking up in Copake just became another day in Hell. Life in Copake had beaten me down, and the farm went into foreclosure. I could have avoided bankruptcy if a sale of my landfill to the county had come through. The county had come to me and wanted to purchase the landfill so they could close it. I gave them a price high enough to keep current with the bank. My old buddy, nemesis Butch Near, probably had a hand in nixing a fair deal for me.

The County hired an appraisal using three land sales some 20 miles distant as comparable sales. I countered with an appraisal of five sales, three adjoining the farm, and the rest within a mile. All the sales were recent and I presented them in the form I learned from my appraisal course at Iowa State University from Doctor Murray. As I recall it figured at just a little higher than my first offer. Just before the foreclosure sale I ended up selling the landfill to the county for two years back taxes. They had me on the run, and the idea that a buyer for the rest of my property would appear at the last moment faded from my mind. The financial problems really started catching up with us, and Cassie's lawyer friend, Burt, advised us to put the Copake house in her name so we wouldn't lose that, too. We followed his advice, and when Cassie later moved to Maine and left me, the house was gone too.

AUCTION, AUCTION

I approached the granite steps of the 1910 courthouse well before the scheduled sale. I thought about my grandfather standing on the same steps years before to have his picture taken as a member of the Board of Supervisors. Inside, along the terra-cotta floors was the marble staircase. People already gathered there for the sale of my farm. Cassie, her daughter and my mother accompanied me. They promised to help save something if they could afford it. As somber as we were, we couldn't help but notice the curious and carnival-like atmosphere of the crowd.

Ben Ackley and his son-in-law were there along with Bob Magley who had just sold 16 acres at $5,000 next to the Brown Farm parcel. And, my brother and nephew showed up too, jovial as hell. My brother visited throughout the room even though we did not speak because of the course of recent events. Victor Myers of the Rapport firm arrived with his young client from Farm Credit who seemed to enjoy his role in the drama about to occur.

At the appointed time the referee mounted the marble steps and announced the sale of the farm in three parcels. The order of sale was set. The first would be the 134-acre flat behind the village. I had refused an offer of $1 million from a developer not long ago so Frank and I could continue farming. It contained the 1 acre that Farm Credit said I had to sell for $30,000 in order for them to release it, and the 20-acre parcel that I had planned to sell for $6,000 before Frank's arrest. After the arrest the price dropped and the Rapport firm advised me not to sell. I figured if bidding started on that parcel first, and it brought half its true worth, I would be able to save the other parcels since it alone would cover the money I owed Farm Credit.

The second parcel was the only one that could keep me in Copake. It included the hill and the greenhouse location on Church Street. Both Cassie and I wanted to save it. A few years earlier a supermarket expressed interest in the location. The last parcel contained the Brown farm. Eileen Cohen, who bought the Brown barn, was there with her lawyer. I wish it had been comforting to know all the people in the room.

Bidding opened on the first parcel as Myers stepped forward announcing the bank's bid of $240,000. The referee asked for further bids and when no responses were forthcoming, he marked it off for Farm Credit. That price was just under $1,800 per acre; the price they got from Odyssey and a good $1,000 below their sell back offer to me. The bad news got worse, and it was clear that we would not be able to retain ownership of the hill and greenhouse property. The bank announced their bid, and then my neighbor bid just a little more and got the sale.

We did put up a fight however. I got into a bidding war for the Brown Farm with my nephew and Eileen Cohen, and together we surpassed the Farm Credit bid. In some states that would have ended the sale. Not in New York. In New York everything is sold and the excess funds are collected by the county. After a time you can reclaim the funds, but you have to pay the county a percentage. I eventually held the edge and was awarded the property.

The trouble with my position reared its head almost immediately when my mother couldn't meet the increased amount of the bid. It burned me when the County Treasurer deducted their fee before he returned my excess funds. After asking for help from Char Peck and my brother, among others, I was forced to sell to Eileen Cohen anyway. All that was left in Copake was the house in Cassie's name, and it was rented. Little by little I moved our things as we painted and papered the Claverack place. Neighbors passed by as my tan pickup with the dented fender loaded furnishings and household goods I had never expected to move.

Just before the sale date, my last load of things was loaded on the truck. I would never return to Copake, the place I grew up and loved. My farm and all I worked for would be gone. I took one more walk down Church Street to the cemetery by the church. There were the graves of A.D. and Liz, of Carl and Grandma Fischer on the left. On my right were the plots of Myers Vosburgh and his father Abram R. Vosburgh. Myers was in the Civil War.

Abram R. took part in the Anti-Rent War. The Anti-Rent war was about land reform. Copake was part of the 160,000 acre Livingston Manor back then. Abram was one of the people dressed as Calico Indians who took papers from Sheriff Miller and burned them in the town square. I have the gun he carried that

December day in 1844. I also have the gun carried by his brother, John, who later moved to Wisconsin.

I walked slowly around and thought of my family heritage that I would leave behind. There was the plot of the Holsapples, Liz's parents. Further on, closer to the church, was the grave of the Van Deusens and Adrian Langdon, A.D.'s grandparent. Abraham Van Deusen settled in Copake in 1687. He was the tenant of Robert Livingston who was Lord of the 160,000 acre Livingston Manor.

Adrian served as a clerk for General Sherman during the Civil War. He got a medical discharge and died quite young. Further along was the smaller stone of his father, John Langdon. He helped his grandson, Grant, get into the store business. Off to the right in the old part of the cemetery were the graves of his father, David Langdon, and his father, John Langdon. John moved to Copake after serving in the French and Indian War. He also served in the Revolution. That headstone was hard to read, and it looked forgotten because of its broken stone. His cousin was also named John, and he had served at the Battle of Bennington and later went on to be Governor of New Hampshire and a signer of the Constitution. It was the same Constitution that promised us freedom and justice and trial by jury.

I went home for the last time with a heavy heart. Disaster was certain and at hand. I climbed into my truck and headed out of town.

FIRES RESUME: THEATER FIRE GETS COPAKE'S ATTENTION

burn and burn and burn

—Charles Bukowski

After the village theater burned to the ground June 14, 1990, all Hell broke loose. CNN News covered the small town with an arson problem. The Independent ran big headlines, "Arson Probe Intensifies," in the June 18 edition. The paper offered a $5,000 reward, and Sheriff Bertram, who followed Paul Proper into office, placed a hotline call-in number soliciting any information that would lead to the apprehension of the arsonist. The County Board of Supervisors offered the "full resources of the county, whatever is needed." I seriously doubted it.

The theater fire really sent the area into a panic, and the public officials appeared nakedly inept to handle the situation. In my mind, if the full resources of the county were put behind a forceful investigation, something might have been accomplished, but in analyzing the politics of it all, I could see that the elected officials would be devastated by an actual finding of the truth.

The lead investigator had not been informed about my suspect, and the DA, Paul Czajka, had not told his own investigator about the burned man reported by Walter Shook's earlier investigation. In addition to the county lawyers who knew about these facts, the chairmen of the Legal Committee were aware of the sheriff's (Proper) actions. It made sense to me that if the arsonist was caught and admitted setting the fire at Bull Spring, the county would be liable for the damages. None of them could have survived that consequence.

Right after the fire, Ben Ackley called a meeting at the Grange Hall to unite the community in an effort to catch the arsonist. Rumors abounded. One identified Henry Call as the suspect. Since he was first on the scene of the fire, people jumped to conclusions. It was like a feeding frenzy once it got started. But Call had taken photos at the Bull Spring fire and he was not the one who got burned. I told everyone I could that was the case, but they didn't want reason, they wanted someone to blame, and they wanted to worry about where the next fire would flair up.

It was a strange experience, having the town gathered together in the 1910 vintage Grange Hall where A.D. once served as Master. I could feel the townspeople's suspicion of Frank as the arsonist from where I sat in the rear of the hall. Ben Ackley and investigator Vick stood up front. Reporters from lots of places including TV Channel 6 were there to cover the event. Ackley called the meeting to order and stated, right off, that the police should have more power. "We need better laws so the sheriffs can't be sued," he said. "They need more freedom to question people."

His remarks seemed to be aimed at me. I knew the police weren't doing what they could be doing now, but I was trying to sue them for damages. I merely had the time to bristle at his remarks before Investigator Vick offered a retort. "We don't need better laws, the laws we have are good enough. What we need are better judges to support the police."

Vick seemed to me to be blaming the judges and my lawsuit for damages as protecting the arsonist. I grew more disturbed. I wondered what Ackley had heard from Vick about my son, Frank. I didn't have long to see how things were going against Frank, and by implication, me. Former Sheriff Proper got up to castigate the community for smearing the good name of Henry Call, saying the rumors had ruined his life in the community. I was rather amazed, to be honest. I had extolled the virtues of Henry Call who took pictures of my fire scene and always distinguished himself as an honest and upstanding member of the community. There was no such similar concern voiced about what was happening to Frank's life and reputation as a result of the false arrest and the subsequent ostracizing and suspicion.

Ackley asked for questions, and someone stood and suggested a neighborhood watch. It was a well spread out "neighborhood" and few people seemed willing to commit the time and effort to making it work. Another suggestion proposed the installation of lights to deter potential arson. My barns were burned in daylight, so the idea of putting in lights fell flat with me. Had a reward been offered? Ackley was vague about it but said it hadn't been done, which wasn't true. I had asked him twice to pledge money to a stop arson fund and he had declined. That part had not really surprised me. Mother always said Ben, our cousin, could never make up his mind and he would never commit himself to anything. It was interesting how after his second fire he changed perspective. Self-interest is a big motivator.

Sheriff Proper called for someone to stand and deliver evidence that would lead to the apprehension of the arsonist. The room was silent as the TV cameras pan the audience. No one stepped forward. Proper again asked for someone to step forward. Again the room was silent. He was convinced someone there knew something significant. He was right. If my lawyer, Steve Cohen, hadn't specifically instructed me to keep out of the fray, I'd have stood and given my story of the burned man and the strong suspicion that George Partridge's hired man was that man. I knew that Arthur Coleman, Jr. had seen the burned man, and that he had reported it, but Sheriff Proper already knew that. The truth lurked about, but no one wanted to shine any light on it. The camera crews from Albany shut down and the story subsided with their departure. As we filed out of the hall, a boy in the crowd asked his mother why the sheriff was mad at the town. I wanted to tell him that the sheriff was deflecting the responsibility to the community when it was he who was supposed to be chasing and catching the criminals. It also seemed to me that Vick had only to find his "better judge" and that it had already been accomplished. Federal District Judge Howard G. Munson was his judge.

A DECADE OF FIRES:
THE INDEPENDENT CHRONICLES
THE BLAZES 1980–90

The Independent, the area's most reliable and accurate news source published a chronology of the fires reported in and around Copake during the 1980–90 decade. The newspaper ran an arson hotline number on the same page with the fire summaries, making the editorial statement of the linkage between cause and effect pretty clear. If the chronology were updated, the news wouldn't be radically different. It's a wonder there are any buildings left to burn in Copake, but even an obsessed arsonist can't put a match to everything, can he?

Fires were listed by date and location in the Independent following the fire that leveled the Copake Movie Theatre on Old Route 22. The chronology lists the most recent fires first and it serves as the information source for this list.

TEN YEARS OF FIRES, MOST NEVER "SOLVED"

- Thursday, June 14, 1990, 3:00 A.M., Copake Movie Theatre, Old Rte. 22
- Thursday, March 22, 1990, 9:10 P.M., Frank's Garage, Church St., Copake
- Wednesday, November 15, 1989, 10:00 P.M., Peck and Peck Funeral Home outbuilding, Church St., Copake
- Tuesday, October 31, 1989, 10:23 P.M., Two family house owned by Dukas, Old Rte. 22
- 11:28 P.M., Brad Peck Insurance Building, Church St., Copake
- 11:33 P.M. Propane gas leak, Grange Hall, Empire Rd., Copake
- Wednesday, August 16, 1989, 11:45 P.M., Barn, Benedict Ackley's Empire Farm, Copake
- Monday, March 27, 1989, 6:12 P.M., Farmhouse apt. Ken Main Farm, Rte. 22, Copake
- Wednesday, January 25, 1989, 3:00 A.M., Brush fire, Peter Bohling, Camphill Rd., County Rte. 7, West Copake
- Wednesday, December 12, 1988, 11:35 P.M., Two story storage barn, A. C. Lumber and Supply Corp., Old Rte. 22, Copake
- Wednesday, November 16, 1988, 1:14 A.M., Two story barn, Brusie Farm, Valley View Rd., Copake
- Tuesday, August 23, 1988, 6:45 A.M., Barn owned by Richard Culley, Dugway Rd., Austerlitz
- Saturday, May 7, 1988, 1:00 A.M., House owned by Marino, Lakeview Dr., Taconic Shores, Copake
- Sunday, April 17, 1988, Fire in the woods, Oleana Campground, West Copake
- Wednesday, December 3, 1987, 9:42 P.M., Fire guts Chevy Blazer owned by D. Hotaling, Copake
- Saturday, October 24, 1987, 2:46 P.M., Garage at Birch residence, Hillsdale

- Monday, September 21, 1987, 9:30 P.M., Vacant mobile home fire, Tripp Farm, Ancramdale
- Monday, August 24, 1987, Barn burned on Schoolhouse Rd., Austerlitz
- Monday, August 17, 1987, Fire in pickup truck owned by T. Miller, Copake Falls
- Tuesday, July 16, 1987, 12:15 A.M., Lumber storage building, Ed Herrington, Inc., Hillsdale
- Sunday, June 28, 1987, 9:18 P.M., Barn on former Niver Farm, Ancram
- Monday, June 15, 1987, 8:08 P.M., Bull Spring Farm barn rented by Mike Langdon from Charles Peck, Copake
- Saturday, June 6, 1987, 10:04 A.M., Storage building, A. C. Bristol Lumber and Supply, Copake
- Thursday, May 28, 1987, 7:41 P.M., Three barns burned, owned by Dorothy Baldwin, Taghkanic
- Saturday, November 15, 1986, 4:50 A.M., Horse barn, Velma Downs, Gallatin
- Thursday, August 14, 1986, 1:10 A.M., Barn, Robert Gilmore Scotland Farm, Ancram
- Wednesday, July 2, 1986, 9:20 P.M., Barn, Ronnybrook Farm (DeLaval Farm), Pine Plains
- Sunday, April 20, 1986, Midnight, Saperstein's Clothing Store, Millerton
- Same weekend, Bob's Clothing and Shoes, Canaan
- Friday, April 11, 1986, 1:12 P.M., Residence, Jenkins Farm, Rte. 22, Copake Falls
- Wednesday, January 9, 1985, 11:30 A.M., House owned by Peter Mollo, Hillsdale
- Saturday, August 24, 1985, 6:58 P.M., Mike Langdon's barn, Church St., Copake
- Sunday, March 10, 1985, Duksa's barn, Lackawanna Farm, Copake
- Sunday, December 11, 1984, 6:45 P.M., Storage Building, Friedman Auction, Copake
- Wednesday, August 1, 1984, 1:44 A.M., Barn, Peter Jensen Farm, County Rte. 7, Ancram
- Tuesday, January 10, 1984, 1:45 A.M., Stephen Lohan's house, Rte. 22, Copake

- Wednesday, January 27, 1983, 2:15 A.M., VFW Hall, Rte. 23, Hillsdale
- Friday, October 15, 1982, 2:10 A.M., William O'Connell garage, Main St., Copake
- Tuesday, October 5, 1982, 9:20 P.M., Horse barn, Buel Peck property, Church St., Copake
- Wednesday, July 14, 1982, 12:36 A.M., Metal barn, George Partridge Farm, Copake
- Friday, January 15, 1982, 3:40 A.M., Home of Karin Mitchell, Rte. 7A, Copake
- Friday, October 23, 1981, 8:02 P.M., Barn burned, William "Beck" Waldorf Farm, Copake
- Saturday, May 23, 1981, 9:30 P.M., Barn, outbuilding, hay, equipment, Frank Lampman, County Rte. 3, Ancramdale
- Sunday, December 11, 1980, 6:45 P.M., Storage building, Friedman Auction, Copake
- Sunday, August 3, 1980, 11:15 P.M., Henry Wemer's horse barn, Copake
- Thursday, July 17, 1980, 1:00 A.M., Mike Langdon's hay barn, Copake
- Tuesday, July 1, 1980, 10:28 P.M., Shed at Peter Miles' Copake Lumber Company, Copake
- Monday, April 21, 1980, 7:00 P.M., Former Ezra Link residence, County Rte. 7, Copake Lake
- Monday, April 7, 1980, Dorothy Bates residence, Ancram
- Thursday, January 3, 1980, 9:30 P.M., Pine Plains Lumber Company, County Rte. 7, Gallatin

For an area the size and population of Copake, one decade's fires could have more normally accounted for half a century's worth. Three fires destroyed property used by Grant "Mike" Langdon for his dairy operation between 1980 and 1987. During the same period the community of Copake devolved from an intimately connected and interdependently caring place to a suspicious and, some might say, self-loathing and alienating town.

MOVING ON

Breaking up is hard to do.

—Burt Bacharach

Working for others proved to be very stressful and unsatisfying. In 1994, I finally found a job with ADM in Hudson, working in a flourmill. My first job put me on a platform where I caught 100-pound bags of flour and stacked them on pallets for shipment. I also spent a lot of time in the basement where the temperatures routinely hit 110 degrees fahrenheit and the constant racket of the rollers drummed out all other sounds.

Besides the mind numbing and physical stress of the job, some of the coworkers could generate pressure for me too. One guy I'll call "Bob" was an ex-felon who developed an intense and obsessive dislike for one of the other workers. In an incident I'll never forget, Bob began acting strangely one night. He would throw his head back and give out a strange laugh while tried to get behind the other worker. All the while he dragged a 4-foot-long steel bar. It looked like something ugly was going to happen so I called two other men into a huddle to discuss the situation. We all agreed that Bob was after the other worker and going to attack. I feared a homicide. The other men could see it coming too. I said we all had to go in together. They agreed so I started out. When I got to where Bob was, I looked back. No one was there.

By this time the worker was scared out of his wits. When I faced Bob he slipped away to safety. That left me standing alone face to face with Bob. He was anything but stable. Since I had just gone through therapy I played the role of therapist and hoped to say the right things that would bring Bob back from the edge. Any violence now would almost certainly be directed at me. I started talking. I remember one of the things I said was what a good forklift driver he was. Bob knew he was good at that. He snapped back to normal as if a switch had been thrown. He dropped the steel bar. By that time the manager appeared and sent everyone home. Later, I was able to talk with Bob about his problems coping with everyday life and his desire to return to prison where he knew what was expected of him. He also told me that he had intended on ramming the steel bar into the coworker's back. I guess that would have landed him back in jail all right. For the other man's sake, I thank God it didn't happen.

We also had times when the trains were late and the mill was in danger of running out of wheat. If we unloaded too late, the bakeries wouldn't get their flour, and I remember putting in 17-hour days to make up the work. There was no way not to sleep good after those days. I finally got the job of "blender" that required shift work. Increasingly, the change in living arrangements and work put stress on the marriage. The loss of the greenhouse business, the terror of the highway incident with the sheriff, and the auctioning off of all my Copake holdings and heritage contributed to a creeping funereal atmosphere that was difficult to shake.

Cassie's Claverack house was one of the historic homes set close to the road across from the old courthouse. It was the same courthouse where Martin Van Buren was admitted to the bar, and even though it's been converted to apartments and the cupola is gone, its front door is the same one traversed by the likes of Van Buren, Alexander Hamilton and Aaron Burr. Cassie's house bears the history of its builders, the prominent Hogenboom family, from the 1700's and maintains the characteristics of its remodeling in 1835. The Federal style features a central hall and four large rooms, each with its own fireplace. With high ceilings and wide hallways to compliment the grand staircase and silver-knobbed doors, the house resembles Van Buren's own house at Lindenwald and is certainly as impressive today as it was in its heyday. But as I sat alone at my desk, the room around me felt strange. It needed new wall treatment and the wide board floor ached to be refinished. Above the desk a strip of wallpaper was Scotch taped to the wall.

After being ruined, it was a struggle to keep going so close to Copake but so far away from my life there. Cassie talked about selling out and leaving Columbia County entirely, and eventually, a buyer turned up for the Claverack house. Cassie found a place in Kennebunkport that she liked and she bought it. Cassie's daughter from New York City bought her mom a new Volvo station wagon that aided in the move to Maine. She also ended up on the deed to my house. I gave up my job at ADM and began looking for work in Maine. I finally found temporary employment as a janitor at the Buxton Town Hall. I was impressed by the openness of government in Maine where boards of selectmen meetings were telecast on cable TV and citizens received annual reports of government business. Government didn't always operate smoothly but it involved the people and what they had to say.

Unfortunately, Maine wasn't far enough away for me not to pick up on rumors of Frank's suspected role as an arsonist in Copake. I submitted a letter of complaint in hopes of curtailing more rumors, but Cassie's lawyer friend got hold of it and threatened a law suit if I didn't stop counterattacking people by name. Cassie, of course, got upset all over again and decided I should spend time with my son Cliff in Toledo, Ohio while I thought things over. It soon turned into a demand, and I acquiesced, starting out after work with a few personal belongings in the car and $200 in my pocket.

I was devastated. I felt like a homeless person. In a fast three years, I lost the house along with job prospects in Maine and my beloved Cassie. Being a farmer, mind you, and a disillusioned patriot, I plodded on like a blind horse. I spent my first night away on my daughter Margaret's couch in Rochester, and then drove on to Cliff's where I stayed in a spare room. I worked a security job for minimum wage for a while. Then when Cliff moved to Cincinnati, I went too. I got a job selling windows, and later, worked in a home improvement store. A string of jobs in a series of stores that eventually failed netted me enough savings to rent my own place, and then I landed a position at Lowe's. That job has sustained me through the dogged process of trying to wring justice from the court system. And, all the while, memories and heartaches from the past went right along with me.

After I arrived in Ohio in 1998, I tried to get the case reopened *pro se* (without a lawyer) based on new evidence. Being without funds, I requested the court help with a lawyer. That request was rejected. I found a letter showing that evidence had been destroyed. I asked the judge to discipline the lawyer involved. My request for discipline was rejected apparently because it was in the form of a letter and not a motion. Resila opposed the new filing in a motion and we sparred in Syracuse before Judge Munson. He wanted the case thrown out again. While I presented the facts of the case, Resila presented case after case of legal precedent. After a year and a half of waiting, Judge Munson ruled for Resila's motion that was heard in Syracuse.

I made a motion for sanctions, this time in the right form. I asked to be heard in a motion to be answered in Albany September 27, 1998. Resila returned papers and I anticipated meeting in Court again. I traveled from Cincinnati to Albany for Judge Munson's court date, but the judge did not show up. Neither did Resila. A call to his clerk brought the answer, he would rule on the motion but doing so in court was not required. Judge Munson ignored it. Finally I was successful in getting a ruling from the Court of Appeals in New York to force Judge Munson to make a decision. The judge claimed the court lost the papers but admitted Resila did return papers. Judge Munson turned down my motion to sanction the lawyers as not timely. No hearing was ever granted. The Court of Appeals in New York upheld Judge Munson's decision apparently based on case law the judge presented. It was as if I were screaming at a deaf man.

Family relationships can be the most painful, and expecting sympathy and understanding from them can cause the greatest of disappointments. My brother's wife flat out told me her position on Frank. "If he didn't do it, why did he sign it?"

Even my father was only passively supportive, and his last word on the situation was "Well, they shut you up." It would have been a big help to me if he and mom had shown up at the hearing before Judge Leaman, but they weren't there.

WHERE ARE THEY NOW

My daughter Margaret is in Rochester. Cliff is back in Toledo where he and his wife Pam have a son, J. T. And Frank still struggles to make a life for himself and his devoted wife, Sara, in Columbia County. A great deal of progress has been made, but life is still hard for them.

Outside my window the trees are budding in the first true signs of spring. I ignore the constant din of traffic just beyond them and reminisce about the hopes of spring in Copake and how much I loved walking through Brown's swamp to check the fences before turning out the heifers. The first wild flowers would be blooming, and the smell of skunk cabbage would be unmistakable. Spring is a time of renewal. It would be bird-nesting time, time to work the soil on the hill for seeding. Stones would have to be picked up, but the long view of the mountains would reward each stretch and bend. When the day was done and the last seed had been sown, satisfaction would soothe sore muscles and I could head for the comfort of the house where Cassie waited to regale me with tales of the greenhouse. I believed it would go on like that, the scenes and smells of Copake fields forever. All these years later, others have moved on too. Friends who lost farms and businesses struggle to make new lives.

Sheriff Proper is enjoying his pension. He didn't run for re-election after Frank's arrest. I believe the reason was that the insurance company would refuse to insure the county again if he did. I guess he used his one false arrest allotment, although he claimed health reasons for not running again. All his legal bills were paid and he did not receive a public reprimand. That allowed him to fulfill the term of Sheriff Bertram after Bertram resigned. Judge Leaman appointed him for the one year left in term that smack of a political deal. It added greatly to his pension benefits from the county.

Investigator Walter Shook went on to run for sheriff on his own. I placed a full-page ad in the Independent outlining his finding in the Bull Spring investigation and his silence later. He maintained his silence on the Bull Spring fire investigation that could have turned up the real culprit, the burning man. The people of Columbia County elected him sheriff but he is now retired and, like his two predecessors, collecting a pension from the county.

District Attorney Czajka seemed to find a calling to go after the Chief of the Hudson Police right after the incident with Frank. He tried to form a County Drug Task Force charged with making all the drug arrests in the county. Only certain officers could make drug arrest. That was supposed to allow the task force to trace the drugs back to the source. Chief Dolen, of Hudson, stood in his way and insisted any police officer should have the right to make arrest and not just the "beefed up" Drug Task Force. Funny thing, after Czajka forced Jim Dolen out of office and got his Drug Task Force, felony drug arrest in the county seemed to fall and the drug problem got worse. Nonetheless Czajka was awarded with a run for judge and was elected. When he ran for reelection I placed a full-page ad highlighting his part in what I call a cover-up to protecting a Republican sheriff. Despite my full-page ad Czajka was reelected by a slim margin. A benefit from the ads, and the big reason I paid for them was that it benefited Frank who still lives in the county. Word seemed to get out he had nothing to do with the fires, he began to experience a lot less trouble and is now a valued member of his new community. Personally, Czajka has not wanted to deal with me and even retreated behind a locked door and told me he didn't want to speak to me one time. I hope being challenged makes him a better judge.

The arsonist was never arrested and is probably still in Columbia County.

Jason Shaw lost his bid for a judgeship by a narrow margin, and he still practices law as a partner in the same very successful Hudson law firm. Tom Griffin left his firm and holds a state job in Albany. Judge Leaman is retired from the bench and practices law.

Gary Greenwald has law offices in Chester, New York, Wurtsboro, New York and West Paterson, New Jersey and as far as I know has many satisfied clients. I understand he teaches law at a local community college and is well liked. He was elected Mayor of his small town.

Judge Munson was cleared of the charges I brought against him yet he seemed to obstruct my access to the court when I tried to collect damages. The VII Amendment guarantees a trial by jury for anything valued at more than $20. The Chief Judge of the Court of Appeals in New York cleared Munson to my enduring distress and a jury trial was never granted. No damages were ever awarded and no apology given. My legal bills exceeded $100,000.

Attorney James A. Resila continues to practice law with Carter, Conboy, Case, Blackmore, Maloney & Laird. They are located in Albany. He serves as a mediator on the Northern District of New York Mediation Panel and is a Barrister in Albany Law School's American Inns of Court.

A trip to Albany to the office of The Committee on Professional Standards proved a waste of time in relation to any complaints I had about any of the lawyers. Their reply was "no cause for action."

Life in a small town is seldom as ideal as we want to remember it. For Copake, the arsonist's identity may never be exposed and the lawyers will probably never be brought to task for their misdeeds. The new sheriff of Columbia County will probably continue to selectively enforce the laws, as sheriffs everywhere probably do. Politics and nonfunctioning courts make it difficult to anticipate much change. What I call "Club Justice" is just too ingrained and too powerful a force. What's the incentive for a lawyer to report a lawyer he must work with every day?

My story is not the only one. This country will belong to us only so long as we fully support our constitutional guarantees. I believe the jury should be more powerful than the judge. I believe our Founding Fathers intended it to be that way. Our Founding Fathers did not trust King George's judges, nor do I think we should fully trust the judges of today. The right to a trial by jury is guaranteed in the Bill of Rights. Because of cost and convenience that guarantee is fast becoming simply words on a document. Lawyers today charge very high hourly fees, but the prosecution has unlimited funds. When it comes to funds for public defenders the story is different. While Jason Shaw was charging me $100 per hour, he was doing the same work as a public defender for the county at the rate of $45 per hour. Then try to get money out of the public defenders office to hire an investigator. Today just a good lawyer can cost $250 per hour or more.

Prosecutors intent on furthering their careers are not hesitant to spend the public's money to win, nor do they feel it is in their interest to be critical of the police. They offer face-saving plea deals when they do not have the facts to support their case as was done in this case. Had I not been able to spend $30,000 just to get ready for trial by hiring the expert I needed, the way the fire started may never have been discovered.

This book is a personal account of what happened to one American living and working in what could be Any Town, U. S. A. At some point in our lives we all are affected by what lawyers do and what happens in the courts. The conditions our lives play out under are governed by the actions we ourselves take. If things go wrong we are the ones that must act. This book contributes to the understanding of the social network I call Club Justice. Club Justice can ensnare anyone. Our courts often make a wrong decision. The new DNA testing that has found many innocent men in jail for rape and murder make my point. In my case the lawyers and Club Justice did more damage than the arsonist that burned three of my barns. They also destroyed my son's life. The public Defender in Columbia County once told me, "We must all get along [in Court] because if we didn't life would be unbearable. We have to work together every day."

There is a way to file a complaint about a Federal District Judge. Under the *Judicial Conduct and Disability act of 1980* a complaint can be filed with the Court of Appeals. The Chief Judge then may do a limited investigation and makes his decision. He is not bared from a thorough investigation at court expense. If his decision is appealed it goes to a Judicial Council appointed from other judges from the Court of Appeals.

When I went to the Justice Department no help was given. When I filed my complaint of lawyer and judicial misconduct in the Court of Appeals it was dismissed. I believe a limited investigation was done which probably consisted of the judge being sent a copy of my complaint for his comment. Some investigation! I believe it was Club Justice at work.

When I appealed the ruling of the Chief Judge in the Court of Appeals the Judicial Council upheld the Chief Judge's decision with days with no further investigation. The fact the Judicial Council did no investigation, made the appeal process meaningless. An investigation by the Justice Department would have un-covered wrongdoing not just of the judge, but of the lawyers. The filing of serious charges by the Justice Department would send a clear massage to the courts that misconduct can be found out, and will not be tolerated.

Recently Chief Justice Roberts of the United States Supreme Court quoted a study commissioned by his predecessor, Chief Justice Rehnquist. Chief Justice Rehnquist wanted to know how the *Judicial Conduct and Disability act of 1980* was working. (The 188 page report by Justice Beyer is available on the Supreme Court Web site.) One of the three reasons that caused a wrong de-cision by the court was that charges of misconduct went uninves-tigated. This did not surprise to me.

Perhaps Justice Roberts will find a way to clip the wings of Club Justice so that charges of judicial misconduct get investi-gated. More likely it will take action by Congress and I intend to send my Congressmen a copy of this book. New legislation is needed to creating a special section of the Justice Department to investigate charges dismissed by the Chief Judge. Judges investi-gating judges is not working. If the complaint is then appealed to the Judicial Council the facts will be provided by the Department of Justice and a proper decision can be made. Judges should not be above the law.

The first step in correcting a problem is to get everyone to agree what the problem is. By defining the problems within our courts we are taking the first step in correcting them. Today our courts do not work and one reason is Judges investigating Judges is not working. This book calls for amending procedures in the *Judicial Conduct and Disability act of 1980* to call for mandatory Justice Department investigations of all decisions of the Chief Judge concerning judicial conduct. With millions of cases going through the Federal Court System each year only about 700 cases of misconduct filed each year. A Justice Department investigation in these cases is reasonable, and would help guarantee the rights granted under the Constitution. My son was arrested for a major crime yet because of a judges decision he never had a trial, but he was in effect pronounced guilty. Judges should not be above the law.

A possible Department of Justice investigation would cause Judges to take more care to see that things are done right. It could affect the way the entire court system works. When the DA discovered Frank was maliciously arrested he opted to cover it up, knowing no investigation would be done. If there was a chance a Justice Department investigation would be done and expose what I see as his misconduct he would have had second thoughts. There has been some discussion as to what should be done in cases of malicious prosecution. One approach proposed would be for the DA to turn it over to the State Attorney General to prosecute. That way the DA could continue to work with the police. It is known to be a problem but the discussion seems to have ended with no action. In the book I even recount a discussion Sheriff Proper had about what happens when a person known to be innocent is arrested. Sheriff Proper was president of the NY State Sheriff Assoc.

The other violations were just as bad, like the destruction of evidence, which I understand is a felony. It was overlooked by Judge Munson. For his part Resila submitted affidavits I believe he knew were not true. If that is so, he should have lost his license and been put in jail.

GRANT DINEHART LANGDON
6243 KINCAID RD.
CINCINNATI, OHIO
45213-1415

6 August 1998

Honarable Howard G. Munson
U.S. District Court
Northern District of New York
P.O. Box 7367
Syracuse, New York 13261-7367

Re; Langdon V Proper, et al
Docket No. 5:98-CV-173 (HGM)(GJD)

Your Honor,

In my presents Steven Cohen of Cohen and Adolph ordered Jason Shaw to turn over everything, and he emphasized it by stating it a second time that he wanted every scrap or shred of material dealing with my son's file.

It is clear by Mr. Shaw's letter of July 1, 1998 that he did not do that. His letter states he instead authorized destruction of some and still has the tape requested by Adolph in his file. Not having this evidence, accumulated at great expense to me, clearly affected my relations with my lawyers and the original case. The file did not show my son did not start the fire nor did it show the results of the psychologist, I paid for, that showed he was not a Pyromaniac.

It is clear by my testimony before this court that the arrest of my son was done for political reasons and the arsonist was allowed to go free for political reasons. It is clear it was improper for Whitbeck to become County Attorney knowing a case for improper arrest was imminent by a client of his firm. It was improper for that firm to withhold and destroy evidence demanded by it's client and his lawyer while serving as County Attorneys. This constitutes obstruction of justice and I request this court address this issue.

Sincerely yours,

_____
Grant Dinehart Langdon, Pro se

cc Shaw, Risela, Frank Langdon, Cohen

RAPPORT, MEYERS, GRIFFEN & WHITBECK
436 UNION STREET
P. O. BOX 36
HUDSON, NEW YORK 12534

TELEPHONE (518) 828-9444
TELECOPIER (518) 828-9719

JOHN J. FASO
OF COUNSEL

MI RAPPORT
TOR M. MEYERS
OMAS G. GRIFFEN
L. G. WHITBECK, JR.
VID L. KRECH
ON L. SHAW

Copy

January 25, 1988

Loss Analysis, Inc.
P.O. Box 28
DeWitt, New York 1321

         Re: Insured: Grant Langdon
               Location: Copake, New York
               Claim No. 87-262

Dear Sirs:

     Please be advised that you have authority to destroy or dispose of the evidence that is being stored by you under L.A.I. Case No. 87-1323.

     Thank you for your assistance in this matter.

                        Very truly yours,

                        JASON L. SHAW

JLS:al